Lil Mueller
349-5729

Slick—the Master Mainstreamer

Warren E. Gerlach

Slick—the Master Mainstreamer

Warren E. "Slick" Gerlach

VANTAGE PRESS
New York

FIRST EDITION

All rights reserved, including the right of
reproduction in whole or in part in any form.

Copyright © 1997 by Warren E. Gerlach

Published by Vantage Press, Inc.
516 West 34th Street, New York, New York 10001

Manufactured in the United States of America
ISBN: 0-533-12060-8

Library of Congress Catalog Card No.: 96-90466

0 9 8 7 6 5 4 3 2 1

To Mom and Dad, who were probably the originators of mainstreaming

Contents

Acknowledgments ix

Prologue 1
1 The Childhood Years 3
2 The High School Years 21
3 My College Years 37
4 My Years in Business 80
5 Activities in Various Service Organizations 114
6 My Family Life 136
7 Living in the Nursing Home 148

Acknowledgments

To Joanne Auinbauh and Brenda Burns who patiently listened to my dictation, worked hard on the revisions and put up with an ungodly amount of my weird sense of humor, sarcasm and so forth

God Love 'em

A special thank you to Dr. Harry James Cargas, Professor of Literature and Languages at Webster University, for his guidance and ideas, that helped me write this book

Slick—the Master Mainstreamer

Prologue

Throughout the book I will try to show handicapped people and their parents how to cope with ordinary living. For the handicapped it is so important to have a sense of humor and to keep a smile on your face. You should never be satisfied and always try for improvement. However, it is important not to try to do something beyond your capabilities. You should always know your place and never make a spectacle of yourself.

In regards to parents of the handicapped, I urge them to push their child to the limit. Although it might take your child ten minutes to perform an ordinary function that you can do in five seconds, let him struggle until he can do it himself. Always try to mainstream your child into ordinary life. Do not send him to a special school even if it would be easier than the ordinary public school. It is important for him to mingle with ordinary children his age and sooner or later they will accept him as one of the gang. When I grew up, although I was as clumsy as an ox, Mom and Dad always let me hang out with the neighborhood gang. Instead of riding a two-wheel bike I rode an oversize tricycle and could go almost anywhere the rest of the gang went. Don't ever let your child feel sorry for himself. Although it is important to discipline your child, always mix it with the proper amount of love. Handicapped people love to be touched and cuddled.

1
The Childhood Years

My great-grandmother Margaretha (born Margaretha Klaus) Weber was born about 1806 at Offenbach near Landau, province of Hesse, Germany. She married George Henry Weber who was born about 1810 at Zeiskman near Landau. They migrated with their six children to the United States.

One of the six was my grandmother, Margaretha. They settled in Karker City, Kansas, where she married Ferdinand Gerlach in December 1867. They had four children: Theodore, Mathilda, Edwin, my father, and Pearl. They moved to Atchinson, Kansas, where her husband, Ferdinand, a barber, died October 15, 1895. My father Edwin was fifteen years old at that time and the family migrated to St. Louis shortly thereafter. In order to support the family, Edwin dropped out of school. He was determined to make something of himself so he went to night school and studied accounting. My father met Oliver Lutteke, my mother's brother, and played tennis with him on the court next to Oliver's house.

My mother, being very skillful and artistic, ran a dressmaking shop on Grand Avenue and Juniata. She had three employees working for her and some of her clientele were the Busches and other prominent families. Mom became acquainted with Dad when he played tennis with her brother, Oliver. Her father, Joseph Lutteke, was a mail carrier. His route consisted of the entire Railway Exchange Building. It was the choicest route and at Christmas he would come home with a load of gifts from the various businesses in the building.

When Dad would play tennis with Mom's brother, Dad became more and more interested in Mom. They always say opposites attract each other and that was certainly true of my parents. My father was a jovial, cool-tempered individual and I never heard him raise his voice except for one day when I walked into his office and heard him try to collect money from one of the printers. Mom, on the other hand, was very strong willed, always expecting perfection, which led to her mental condition in later years. Mom's sister, Aunt Blanche, tells of walking to school with Mom. Whenever Mom didn't get her own way she would sit down in the gutter and scream. People, including my father, always gave in to her. The more people gave in to her the more strong willed she became.

My mother and father married July 25, 1914. For nine years they had a rather carefree life. They became good friends with Dr. Al Hertel and his wife, Lydia. Dr. Hertel's practice was in the same building where my mother's dress shop was and Dr. Hertel loved to play practical jokes. During this period my father gave up his job on commission row in the flower business and, along with several other men, formed the Acme Paper Company, at 115 South Eighth Street. He became the secretary/treasurer of the company and held that job for thirty-eight years before he retired in 1948.

After being married for nine years they must have had quite a celebration on Christmas Day 1922, because I was born exactly nine months later on September 25, 1923. My father was forty-four and my mother was thirty-seven years old at the time of my birth and she had a difficult time. Dr. Hertel attended at the birth.

When Mom gave birth to me something went wrong. Probably forceps were used and too much pressure was applied. At that time my handicap was known as Little's Disease. It was named after a doctor in England. Not until 1937 was it given the name of cerebral palsy. This condition, caused by brain damage, can effect any part of the body—sometimes only in one arm or one side or one leg. Fortunately, the pressure on my brain was equally distributed causing me to be spastic all over my body. The doctors said that I would probably never walk or speak and all my life it has been fun to prove them wrong. One break I got was not having my mentality harmed in any way. Some people might argue over this subject. The private nurse, Miss Dewey, who took care of me and Mom at the time of my birth, became a friend of the family for life. From the time the doctors were pessimistic about my future capabilities, Mom was out to prove them wrong and did everything in her power to mainstream me into every possible situation.

I was given the name of Warren in all probability because, at the time of my birth, Warren G. Harding was president. Even during that early administration there was a scandal when Albert Fall, Secretary of the Interior, made personal profit from the sale of oil leases at the navy yards at Teapot Dome, Utah. This is where the expression, "He is the fall guy" originated. It seems rather stupid to me why one administration did not learn from the other because since that time every presidency has been marred with some type of scandal caused by a greedy official. I might add that Woodrow Wilson, who preceded Harding, wanted our country to join the League of Nations. Congress, however, overruled him because the members of Congress did not want ever again to send our troops into foreign lands. Just think if we had joined the League of Nations and put our forces behind it, maybe Adolph Hitler, Joseph Stalin, and Mussolini would not have attained the power and influence they had. Maybe we would not have had to send our troops all over the world as we did and are doing today. Just think of all the money that all the countries have spent on wars. If these funds would have been applied to food, medicine, housing, and education for the poor the world today would be much more civilized in all respects.

After my mom and dad were married they lived on Alberta Street, one block from my mother's parents' flat. After several years they moved to the first floor of a three story flat owned by my father's sister, Mathilda (Aunt Tillie), at 3510 Pestalozzi Street. Whenever a policeman arrested someone on Pestalozzi Street they would drag him over to Holiday Street to avoid having to spell Pestalozzi. We lived at the west end of Pestalozzi, one block from Tower Grove Park. On the east end of Pestalozzi was the Anheuser Busch Corporation. Just think if Dad had bought 800 shares of Anheuser Busch stock at that time it would be worth thousands and thousands of dollars now. It is the same old story of hindsight being better than foresight.

Mom and Dad lived on the first floor, Grandma Gerlach and Aunt Pearl (Dink) lived on the second floor and Aunt Tillie lived on the third floor. Our first floor flat on Pestalozzi consisted of a living room, dining room, bedroom and small hall room where I slept. My bedroom had a small window facing a brick wall ten feet away. On hot nights before we had the rear porch screened I threw a blanket on the floor in the front hall and got whatever breath of air I could. In the bathroom we had an old-fashioned claw-foot bathtub. When I was small Dad would get in the tub with me and scrub me down every Saturday. Saturday was also hair washing night. Mom would put me in front of the hot air register and it made me breathless. Of course, when I was really small Mom would give me a soaking in the kitchen sink. Off the kitchen was an old-fashioned pantry. How I loved to climb up and arrange the cans. When Mom and Dad went out for the evening Aunt Tillie would come and put me to bed.

Dad's sisters were Mathilda (Aunt Tillie) and Pearl (whom I called Dink). Aunt Tillie worked in Albert Terry's real estate office along with her sister Dink. One fall afternoon on the day of the Veiled Prophet Parade, Mr. Terry was home in the afternoon. Since he never left the office, Aunt Tillie was sure he was the Veiled Prophet for that year. Dink only worked a few years and then she stayed home and kept house for Grandma Gerlach. Aunt Tillie was very successful in the real estate business and made a tidy sum by taking over second mortgages. Of course, that would be a hard thing for me to do because I couldn't throw somebody out of their house. However, someone had to do it. It is just one of those difficult things which occur every day.

Aunt Tillie owned a big Reo and drove her mother and sister out for a ride every Sunday morning. As fate would have it, in 1936, Aunt Tillie died on the third floor of the flat of pneumonia with a nurse who kept the windows wide open in ten degree weather. This was the typical way of handling pneumonia in those days before penicillin came on the market. Her sister, Pearl, refused to enter her sister's sick room in fear of getting pneumonia. Nothing was sadder to me than to have her die under such conditions, since she left nearly a quarter of a million dollars, which is equal to about a million dollars today. I won't ever forget going to the cemetery on a cold, snow-covered day in January. I distinctly remember the clank, clank of the chains on the tires of the limousine.

The other member of the Gerlach family was Dad's brother, Uncle Teddy (Theodore) and his wife Aunt Cora. They were rather distant and the only time we met with them was at Thanksgiving dinner which was always held at Aunt Tillie's and Aunt Pearl's. My father was the chief turkey carver. Only recently did it dawn on me they were actually my aunt and uncle.

Uncle Teddy owned a jewelry store on the corner of Euclid and Enright. One summer evening four men knocked on the back door and held them captive. Two men stayed with Aunt Cora while the other two men marched Uncle Teddy over to his store, which was about three blocks away. They warned Uncle Teddy not to do anything foolish. After this horrifying experience and loss of many dollars, Uncle Teddy was never the same and became quite a recluse.

Aunt Blanche, my mother's sister, worked at the post office and met a young man named Henry Patrick McKenna. He also worked at the post office. It was a coincidence that my Irish uncle's birthday was on March 16 and my German dad's birthday was on March 17—they should have been reversed. Being Irish my Uncle Harry was a Catholic and my Aunt Blanche became a devoted converted Catholic. For the last nine years before she died Aunt Blanche constantly held her rosary beads. I thought it was so apropos that she died on Good Friday at the age of ninety-eight on April 13, 1979, and was buried on Easter Monday. At her grave site I was rather aggravated when the priest, from the nursing home, walked over to me and asked me for a donation to the home where she had been for fourteen years. When her funds were depleted I paid for half of her expenses for five years.

Mom's brother, Oliver, who was responsible for Mom and Dad meeting, was a refrigerator car salesman for the railroad. He and his wife, Laura, and their young son, Oliver, moved to New Orleans for a few years because of business. When Uncle Oliver lost one of his kidneys, Laura divorced him and he moved back to St. Louis. In order to support his son, Uncle Oliver bought a rooming house on the corner of Westminster Place and Vandeventer. The house was quite ornate and had many rooms. He used the front room for his own as a combination living, dining, bedroom and kitchen. The room could be compared to a room like Fibber McGee and Molly's closet. I have never seen such a jumbled room in all my life. Because of his kidney problem he couldn't work and rented out ten or twelve of the rooms. Being of ill health, Uncle Oliver went to a movie for a quarter almost every afternoon. This was his only pleasure outside of telling wild stories about some of his tenants who were real characters. They were mostly transient people who came and went like fleas. Uncle Oliver rented rooms for five dollars a week and he could tell stories about many of the tenants. He let his son, little Ollie, use one of the rooms. Ollie attended Central High School and sold newspapers on the corner of Newstead and Vandeventer for two cents a piece. My cousin Ollie received 3/4 cent for each paper he sold. I always admired my cousin for coping under such conditions. He was a hard worker and well-mannered individual. His first job was being a dock hand on the old Mississippi River. Ollie worked under all kinds of conditions and often had to work twelve-hour shifts.

In those days, he bought and ate a blue-plate special for thirty-five cents. After working on the docks for seven or eight years, Ollie was employed by the Mississippi Valley Barge Line which was later bought out by the Chromalloy Company. Upon Ollie's death his wish was granted and his ashes were spread over the Mississippi River.

I do not remember much until I was five years old. Up until that time I was carried and given tender loving care. The neighborhood we lived in was considered South Side Dutch. Every Monday morning everyone hung out their wash after they put it through the hand-operated wringer. Tuesday was ironing day. Friday was cleaning day and on Saturday the good old Germans would scrub their wooden or stone steps. All the lots were thirty-five feet wide and divided by fences. Everyone had their flower gardens on both sides of the fences and took pride in their flowers. At the rear of each lot was a concrete ash pit which was emptied by the ashman. I am proud to say that the neighborhood is still well kept. Our house was two blocks from a shopping area on Grand which had almost every kind of store that you would find in the modern-day mall. All they would have to do to the two block area is add one roof over all and install air conditioning and they would have had a modern-day mall. Everyone says nowadays that we are living in a service-oriented society. In my opinion they sure didn't know about the olden times. In those days the milkman, vegetable man, and iceman came down the alley daily and the White Bakery delivery man came to the front door twice a week. When you were ill the doctor would come to your house. The department stores also made daily deliveries and the postman came twice a day. Local letters cost two cents and out of town letters cost three cents and postcards were one cent. During the Christmas card season three deliveries were often made in the morning and two in the afternoon. Would you rather have the old days back or are you happy to pay more for all of your modern conveniences?

During my infancy, Dad developed an alcohol problem. Fortunately he went to Alcoholics Anonymous and he didn't stop cold turkey, he stopped cold elephant! He would never accept a cocktail, a can of beer or a sip of wine until his dying day forty years later. During this period Dad took instruction in the Masonic Lodge and this also helped him with his alcohol problem.

Mom and Dad became members of the Christian Science Church and every time they had an ailment they would call Mrs. Skidmore and she would pray for them morning and evening. She lived in a swanky apartment and played bridge every afternoon. We would contact her morning and evening and note our improvement. I often wonder whether her prayers were any stronger than ours. She charged a daily fee and in one way I thought it was a scam. Christian Scientists did not believe in medical intervention. Thank God I didn't get appendicitis during those years. Christian Science is a religion of positive thinking. The book, *Science and Health* by Mary Baker Eddy is a great book to read and follow. However, you must be practical in your interpretation. Only a few weeks ago there was a spinal meningitis outbreak at Principia, a Christian Science College. They allowed two students to die before the County was given permission to vaccinate the other students. Some members of the church let their precious children die and because of our freedom of religion granted by the constitution they are never prosecuted. I ask my readers, don't you think practicality comes before morality in these cases? Christian Science argues that it is God's will but would they ever think that they could be robbing society of our future scientists, inventors, and leaders? There is a commandment, "Thou shalt not kill." Should they be tried for neglect of their children just like many people are when they do not care for their children properly?

My earliest memories are around age five when I began taking my first steps. I can remember falling down once and thinking, *I will never walk again.* After a little practice I learned to keep one foot from stumbling over the other and Aunt Tillie would give me a quarter every week that I didn't have a scab on my knee. As I grew older my mother, trying to mainstream me, insisted that I play with the neighborhood gang. Because we played in the alley I ground many pieces of brick into my knees. At the age of six I began to speak. I always had trouble with "H's" so it was very difficult for me to say "heck" or "hell."

At the age of five, Mom and Dad visited the Elias Michael School for Crippled Children on the corner of Euclid and Forest Park. Mr. Stephens, the principal, carried me around and introduced Mom and Dad to Mrs. Farrar, the kindergarten teacher, who told them I would get along fine. Consequently, the bus picked me up every morning and brought me back every evening. I dare say that it could have been the first busing of students.

Each bus had a driver and a female attendant for the students. These men and women served as aides to the students during the day. My seat mate was Edwin Earsom, a lifelong friend. He had infantile paralysis and wore braces on his legs and a back corset for support. He walked with crutches. Each morning his two brothers and father would carry him out to the bus. His father was a strict minister and he always frowned on the card parties my mother and the other mothers of the school conducted for funds to improve the school. I am so proud that Ed became a lifelong friend. Ed received his master's degree in music and along with teaching music and biology, he led a band in Bixby, Oklahoma, for many years. Ed married a teacher in the high school and they raised a son and daughter. Ed's wife, Jo, was a dear and understanding girl. For many years I stopped at their house and spent a night with them on my way home from Oklahoma City where I often visited friends. Ed always allowed me to address his afternoon classes and I always tried to point out what it meant to be an American. Ed and Jo are now retired and enjoying the fruits of their labor.

The Elias Michael School was built exactly square. Its classrooms were on the outside and the inside of the building contained a stage area, a meeting room and a small play area. The lunch room was also in the inside square. Almost every student had infantile paralysis or a similar handicap. These students were given daily physical therapy. Since little was known about cerebral palsy, the few cerebral palsy students that were in the school did not receive any treatment. In the past ten years they have learned that if you begin therapy at an early age cerebral palsy children develop more use of their arms and legs. However, I took speech therapy from Mrs. Bartlett. She taught me how to breathe and I had the pleasure of saying "heck" and "hell."

In kindergarten, Mrs. Farrar taught me the colors of the rainbow and I played with blocks, etc. Mrs. Bowen, a motherly gray-haired woman, taught the first grade. Our first lesson of the day was always learning to read. I was way ahead of everybody and she would never call on me. Ms. Devlin, a wiry young woman, taught second and third grade and I progressed nicely. At that early age I kept quiet whenever she left the room while the other students cut up. Mrs. Bergman wore thick eye glasses and taught the fourth grade, where I learned my multiplication tables and long division faster than anyone else. Miss Easley, a young spry woman, was my fifth-grade teacher and I was her star pupil. This is the first time I remember being taught geography. Fortunately, my only reason for learning quickly was that I was blessed with a high IQ.

During this period in my life Dad became president of the PTA and Mom chaired the annual picnic. This event was held at Tower Grove Park on a day in June. The buses were decorated and arrived in the park about 9:30 A.M. Each pupil was given ten tickets which they could use for food, fish pond or other activities. I looked forward to this annual event and I can remember having dreams about it throughout the years. At Christmas Santa Claus always came in with gifts and treats for the children. When I finished the sixth grade the young Jewish teacher, Marion Strauss, told my parents that they should let me take the sixth grade over. That way I could stay in school that much longer. My mom politely told her to go to hell and withdrew me from school. However, Ms. Strauss kept track of my accomplishments and sent me a Christmas card for years and always praised my successes. This direct action my mom took was the first step in mainstreaming me into everyday living.

By the fall of 1994 the Board of Education of St. Louis acquired a large tract of property where a housing development was torn down. They are now constructing a three building complex. One building will be a regular grade school, one building will be a regular high school and the third building will be a new Elias Michael School for Crippled Children. The object of doing this is to let the handicapped students attend regular school as much as possible while at the same time receiving physical therapy. This is an important part of mainstreaming handicapped people.

Since we were Christian Scientists at that time my parents tried to enroll me in the seventh grade at Principia School on Page Avenue. I was not accepted because they claimed that I had not made a complete demonstration. They said that my physical condition would cause the other students to lose faith in their religion. Come on guys—how would they expect injured muscles to be repaired through prayer. Now I think they could have handled the situation by showing the students how much I improved every year and just tell them that muscles are out of God's control. However, the head master of Principia High School agreed to give me private lessons from five to six every afternoon. Fifteen minutes for English, fifteen minutes for math, fifteen minutes for science and fifteen minutes for social studies. Consequently, Mom drove me out to the school every afternoon. While driving to and from Principia the news was about King Edward and his decision to marry a commoner, Wallis Simpson. He gave up the throne to marry the woman of his dreams. Since you read so much about the escapades of the royal family, maybe a commoner would have brought civility to the royal family. As my friend, Nick, would say, they all got to go to the toilet and wipe their bottoms the same way as everybody else.

The following day I would study by myself and prepare for the next evening. By studying by myself I developed excellent study habits which benefited me throughout high school and college. Mr. Remington was a rather staid individual and a very strict Christian Scientist—in fact he went so far as to deliver their five children by himself.

During my grade school years Mom and Dad did a great job in mainstreaming me with the children of the neighborhood. I learned to throw a ball, pitch rubber horseshoes, and participate in most children's activities. Aunt Tillie had the side yard covered with concrete so we could play ball. We also shot marbles on the grass in the yard beyond the concrete. Naturally this spot became quite worn and was cause for a little agitation by my upstairs relatives that we were ruining the yard.

During this era there was a specialist in New York City who was working in the cerebral palsy field. Mom and Dad asked Aunt Tillie to fund the bill for my trip. She flatly refused. I really don't know how much good the trip would have improved me but with Aunt Tillie being well to do the refusal caused hard feelings off and on for many years to come.

Dad purchased a small pedal car for me to ride in and as I grew up they purchased a three-wheel bike which I rode all over the neighborhood. Can you imagine, I used to ride in the alleys across Grand Avenue and go into Tower Grove Park. Fortunately there was not as much traffic in those days as there is now. Also during this period I would go over to the corner at night and wait for Dad to get off the bus. While doing so Mr. Rebbe, the corner grocer, would allow me to straighten the shelves in his store. I always had an urge to keep things straight, even to this day. At home one of my favorite things was to climb up in the pantry and straighten the cans. Mom couldn't stand to be teased and I will never forget one day when I was teasing her she thought I was giving her sass and she really whacked my face. I fortunately caught the point and went easy from then on. My father on the other hand was my pal and buddy. He loved to take a wet wash cloth and sting my rear end. One morning on

April 1, he rushed into my room and said, "Warren, it's snowing." Of course it was a good April Fool's joke. He took me to many ball games at Sportsman's Park. Dad took me down to the office on Saturday mornings and let me ride on the delivery truck, play with the adding machines and push the empty carts around the warehouse. My continual remembrance of Dad was when he sat at his desk smoking and cleaning his pipe. The spittoon at his desk came in very handy. Every week Dad would bring me a box of small slabs of chocolate from the Busy Bee Candy Company. On the 4th of July Dad and I would sit in the gutter and shoot firecrackers. In the evening we would go over to Aunt Blanche's and Uncle Harry's and light sparklers. Every first of December, Mom and Dad would drape the archway between the living room and dining room. From that time until Christmas they would work in the living room building a fantastic Christmas scene made of cardboard boxes and starched cloth. Dad took care of the train's platform and mechanical problems. On Christmas Eve when Santa Claus came we would pick up Aunt Blanche and Uncle Harry and while we were gone Santa Claus took down the drape and put all the gifts around the tree. Now I know that Aunt Pearl performed this function.

These were the days of Joe Medwick, Pepper Martin, Frankie Frisch and the Dean brothers, who were famous ball players of the St. Louis Cardinals. On hot afternoons in the summer I would lie down in front of the radio and listen to Ma Perkins, Pepper Young's Family and Stella Dallas. The sound effects of Pepper being caught in a storm were almost as good as seeing it on television.

Our first car was a Star which had to be cranked to start, and in a few years we acquired a Mormon. Walter Jenneman, Jack Robbins and I stuck together. Walter was the grandson of Mrs. Beckemeier, who was the widow of the owner of the Beckemeier Lumber Company. She was quite wealthy and lived with the Jenneman family and owned the most pretentious house in the neighborhood. It was a very spacious three story house with big hallways and four or five bedrooms. One summer Walter and I had a clubhouse in the basement built out of cartons. On the opposite side of the coin was Jack who lived with his mother who struggled to support him by working as a clerk at Sears Roebuck. Mrs. Robbins was a jolly person and she did a wonderful job raising Jack. He and his mother lived in a three room second-story flat on Arsenal Street, one block from Walter on Crittenden Street, which was one block from Pestalozzi Street where I lived. Unfortunately Jack went to war and was killed while being a bombardier in World War II. Later in life Mrs. Robbins held a little grudge against Walter who survived. I visited her a few times when I was in my thirties and as I became busier and busier I stopped visiting her and regretted it. Last year a nurse called me and said she wanted to report the death of Mrs. Hartig (Robbins). The nurse said she had followed my life and spoke about me almost weekly.

Walter became another lifelong friend. He married a wonderful woman and they have a son and daughter. Walter was a mining engineer and to this day he is called upon for advice when drilling an oil well. Recently Walter visited me and when I told him that my only bad investment was $50,000 I lost in an oil venture, which guaranteed me fourteen percent income for two years and then became worthless, Walt said "Join the party, I've lost money in the oil business myself."

At this point of my life I am getting into a very sensitive happening but I feel that I should comment on it since it affects so many handicapped people. Mom or Dad never talked about the birds and bees so consequently I had to find out for myself. My first sexual experience happened very suddenly when one of my friends showed me about the birds and bees. You could call it a modified rape but I was scared to death. I never told Mom about the experience because she would have blown the neighborhood apart. Masturbation has been a very relaxing part of my life. I want everybody to know that handicapped people have the same instincts, feelings and desires and want to be loved. Therefore, if you have a handicapped child I urge you to see to it that he or she has a very satisfying sex life as any other ordinary person.

At the beginning of 1937 Dad received his share of Aunt Tillie's estate. He bought mutual funds and property at 54 Webster Acres in Webster Groves, Missouri. At that time the councilmen of Webster Groves were very adverse to having businesses in the city. They could have annexed the property that is now Crestwood, a thriving community which has a huge business area including a modern-day shopping mall, which provides the city of Crestwood with enormous tax revenues. Because of their failure to see the future, Webster Groves citizens are now burdened with a high tax rate for their schools.

Mom and Dad decided to build a house on the lot on the hill of the inner circle of Webster Acres. Our house was a two-story, frame-and-brick house with a two-car garage underneath. The driveway into the garage was surrounded by the high retaining wall. You really had to maneuver the car back and forth before you could come out. Of course, we followed the construction of the house very closely. As in most houses the hole that was excavated for the foundation seemed so small but as we came out nightly we could enjoy the walls going up, the roof going on, the inside woodwork being added and many of the other features of the house. We moved in on July 25, 1937, which was Mom and Dad's thirty-third wedding anniversary.

2
The High School Years

During the first week of August, the secretary of the principal at the high school, Miss Ridgeway, who lived across the street from our new home, questioned my mother on when she was going to enroll me in the junior high school.

Mom replied, "Warren has a private tutor and I drive Warren every day to his tutor."

Ruth said, "Come on, give Warren a chance. I think we could handle him at Webster High."

Since Mom was always trying to mainstream me into ordinary living she jumped at the chance. A few days later we met with the principal of the junior high, Mr. Howard Latta. It was a beastly hot day. When Mr. Latta took us up on the third floor of the high school building to meet my future home-room teacher, King "Barney" Barnett, he was preparing for his biology class for the beginning of the term. Barney was stripped to the waist and I'll never forget the look on his face. He was embarrassed beyond words. (May I sidestep from my tale and tell you that Barney is now ninety-two years old and has followed my life with keen interest.)

The opening day of school I met Jim Cutter, who was a classmate in my home room. He took me under his wing. All through high school Jim got my lunch and after school in the early years we went to each other's houses and played board games since I was not able to participate in outdoor sports. In our senior year Jim worked on the high school newspaper staff and I worked on the high school yearbook staff. We both enjoyed our work and benefited greatly from the contacts we made. After graduation, Jim entered Washington University Medical School and had this education interrupted by the war. However, true to form, Jim stuck with his education and after the war he finished medical school and became a well-known anesthesiologist. Throughout the years, Jim was requested to give lectures throughout the country.

Although Jim was raised a Congregationalist, he fell in love with the sweetest, softest-spoken person I ever met. Her name was Norma and she was a Catholic. Although Jim and I had kidded about the Catholic religion throughout high school, when Jim married Norma he turned Catholic and took his new religion very seriously. In fact, to prove my point, Jim had seven children, all of which turned out to be outstanding kids. If I remember correctly, Jim had four boys and three girls. One is now a doctor, two are experts in the computer field and one is an outstanding businessman. True to their parents' upbringing, they all are having large families (fifteen grandchildren to date) and Jim and Norma moan when they all come home for the holidays. The children sleep on the floor and on whatever else is available.

Throughout Jim's life I have visited him in many places, including Biloxi, Mississippi; Buffalo, New York; Oklahoma City, Oklahoma; and San Francisco and Moraga, California. I had my last great trip when I flew to Frisco and Jim took a week off and showed me the town. During the week we ate at Fisherman's Wharf, went to the Top of the Mart, drove down Highway 1 which follows the coastline of the Pacific Ocean, and spent a day in

Napa Valley. It was a wonderful way to end my travels and I will be eternally grateful to Jim for the week he devoted to me. A few years later Jim and Norma came to St. Louis to visit me. One of the highlights of his visit was when we visited Ruth Ridgeway who was responsible for me entering Webster High School. To this day when I speak with Jim I always ask Jim how Norma is. Although they are still madly in love Jim always says, "The old battle ax is as crabby as ever." My life has been greatly enriched by being a close friend with Norma and Jim throughout the years.

While in home room every morning I would straighten out Barney's outside reference books, which he kept stacked in a closet. Barney kept a beehive outside his window and one morning while sitting in the home room one of his pet bees took a liking to one of my nostrils. Barney ran over and got the bee out before it did any damage.

All my classes went pretty well but when I got home the first day I guess I cried a little from nervous tension, but after that everything was peaches and cream. I did the normal eighth grade courses and the only complaint I have is that Ms. Essig, my English teacher, who I had at the last hour of the day, held the entire class back five or ten minutes after school when a few classmates would misbehave. This was her way of controlling the class, but since I was well behaved and never caused her any trouble I thought her practice was very unfair and burned my posterior.

During my eighth grade, the assistant principal, Mr. Aldrich, and Barney met with Mom and Dad at our home to discuss what track at the high school I should follow. Both Barney and Mr. Aldrich smoked big black cigars and my Dad felt quite at home with them. Because they knew I had a rather high IQ, they outlined the hardest courses they could, including four years of Latin, four years of math and four years of science. I was excused from chemistry because the teacher, Doc Schultz, was afraid I might injure myself or blow up the whole school. During the eighth grade the only modification they made for me was to let me out five minutes early to go to lunch so I wouldn't have to fight the mob. After the first year my pal, Jim, always put my lunch on his tray and we ate together throughout the high school years. My social studies teacher, Ms. Brantley, gave me an oral test every time she gave a written test to the other students. We would sit in front of the class and speak in low tones. My general science teacher was Mr. Case, a young teacher who could teach expertly. Mrs. White, my eighth grade math teacher, was on her last leg. Each day she would teach math for fifteen minutes and then read stories for the rest of the period. Someone reported her and she was replaced the following year. In the ninth grade, I began my long association with the dead language, Latin, and I carried my typewriter from class to class and used it for every test. Ms. McClain taught the primary factors of the language, including verbs, various verb tenses, etc., in preparation for my tackling of the advanced Latin classes taught by Ms. Hazel Farmer. During this year I became a hall monitor during the lunch hour and wore an orange band around my right arm. Of course, at that young age it made me feel like a big shot. The same year I was chosen by the teachers to be a member of the Junior Honor Society.

On Monday evenings, for various purposes, I attended a Hi-Y meeting comprised of young boys. Our leader must have been involved with several of the boys. He was forced to resign and no further action was taken.

Only a few persons knew of the reason for his resignation, because in those days we did not have eager reporters or TV coverage to pick up on sex deviates.

One of the teachers that I remember vividly was Ms. Farmer, my Latin teacher. She assigned us thirty lines of Caesar, Cicero, and Virgil every night. She started out with about thirty-five students in Caesar and by the time we got through Virgil twelve remained. I was one of the ones that endured the routine. Ms. Farmer had Latin running out of her ears. She sponsored the Latin Club and published a monthly Latin newsletter, and always threw a big banquet at the end of the year. I always wondered what she did with her spare time. All of my teachers were tickled to have me in their classes and always marveled at my progress.

While I was in the tenth grade I was inducted into the Quill and Scroll Society which was for students who showed an ability for outstanding writing. The following essay was one of my many essays which qualified me for the organization:

What Americanism Means to Me

America! America! That name alone reaches the core of my heart, when I hear it repeated. Sometimes it makes me shout and rally with all the vigor that I can exert. At other times when that sacred word reaches my ears, I am overcast with a shadow of reverence, and my knees automatically bend towards the ground. When a thing can produce two exactly opposite emotions in a human being, it is a power to be marveled. Yes, Americanism is one of the few sacred powers of the world. No other "ism" looks after the rights of the people, the security of its citizens, or the affairs of a complicated business organization. Therefore, let us peek into the inner realms of this omnipotent phrase.

Life! We speak; we see; we live! Are we bound by the dictates of one supreme leader? Yes, we live under the most powerful dictator of any country in the world. But let us be thankful that our leader has not a mustache or a lock of black hair hanging in his face. Our leader is shapeless and possesses no mortal continuity. From this, we gather that mortal appearance means practically nothing at all; but that it is the spiritual power that counts. If it wasn't for that supreme power, none of us would be enjoying our lives in America today. Have you ever thought of who created our scenery: the mountains, valleys, rivers and falls. Now, of course, after you have been reminded, all Americans will say God. Yes, he did this, and he will do many more things. If we all hold the right thought, he will see that the Grand Canyon, Old Faithful, and the Royal Gorge will stand, undisturbed by the works of mortal hands. Not only this, but he will let us stand by these great wonders, and let us say that these marvels, which inspire all Americans, are ours, the property of us all, Americans.

Liberty! In America we do have freedom; and no other nation can surpass us in this field. To me our liberty is enveloped in two great masterpieces, namely, our Flag and the Statue of Liberty. When I see the American Flag unfurling itself with the wind, whether it is at the national capitol or in front of our school, the same trend of thought always grasps my mind. Why? Why should I always retain the same thought? The answer, as I see it, is that wherever our flag lifts its undaunted stars, there is liberty for everyone—tramps to millionaires, Christian Scientists to Catholics, and Germans to Americans. The flag in front of our school certainly emphasizes my point. In our educational establishment there are eighteen hundred students; each one with the same right as the other. They do not quarrel with each other over religion, they are not concerned from what country our great grandfathers came from, and they are not taught the thoughts of one individual. Again, I ask why? And again I'll tell you that the answer is that they are all Americans, endowed by their creator with certain unalienable rights. Liberty is not confined within our school; but it reaches out to every corner of America. In our homes we can hear the viewpoints of our fellow comrades over the radio, in our office we can read the newspaper editorials, severely knocking our fearless leader, and in our travels we can see such marvels as the Golden Gate Bridge and the Statue of Liberty. Yes, from any part of our huge nation we can travel over well-constructed roads and bridges; and end up at the Statue of Liberty. There it stands in the bay of a great metropolis, the savior of all the oppressed people of the world. With outstretched hands it beckons every nationality, creed, and race, and says: "Come to me, I will protect thee from all the sorrow and strife of the world." This is America. Are you proud to be an American?

The Pursuit of Happiness! Happiness! Every American citizen should be happy; not because the Declaration of Independence says so, but because we are Americans. The Declaration of Independence did not present us with happiness; on the other hand it said that every American had the right to go after it. That is a challenge—if there ever was one—to pursue happiness. Of course, we, as Americans, have something to be joyous about; and therefore our task is half completed. Why shouldn't Americans be happy? They have more than any country in the world and enjoy more freedom than any other people. Well, I think most Americans are happy and glad that they live in America. A few hold personal grudges, a few are born crabby, and a few just don't care. I suppose that these different types of people all go to make up such a balanced country as America. As peace-loving Americans we ought not to be so grateful that we have happiness, but that each and every one of us has an equal right to make happiness a part of us.

As you can see by now that Americanism signifies to me the right to indulge in Life, Liberty and The Pursuit of Happiness; and that I, as an American, am deeply grateful that I am one.
Warren E. Gerlach, 11th Grade Student

In the eleventh grade I received the American Legion cup for being the outstanding student in American History. I think I flustered the man presenting the award. I stuck out my hand to shake his but he just walked off the stage and left me cold. I progressed in high school and made As and Bs and I was inducted into the National Honors Society in the eleventh grade. Most of the students were not inducted until they were seniors.

During my senior year Mr. Newton "Uncle Newt" Settle, sponsor of the yearbook, selected me to head the circulation for the yearbook. There were only eighteen students on the whole staff that met every day at the last hour of school. Uncle Newt was a fun, teasing man and I really enjoyed being on the yearbook staff.

The editor of the yearbook that year was Bob Copeland who later became my lifelong friend and served as my lawyer until his death. Bob worked very closely with Uncle Newt, who was the teacher that impressed me most throughout my life. Bob Copeland was set in his ways and ready to face the world. After the service he completed his undergraduate and law degrees at Washington University, graduating first in his class from the Washington University Law School. In 1953 he was the youngest state representative ever elected in Missouri. He served three consecutive terms and during the last of those married Pat, a registered nurse. Bob's father was administrator of Missouri Baptist Hospital. I could give you story after story about the funny things Uncle Newt pulled but one of the funniest was the time he sent my name as a prospective student for St. Mary of the Wood, a Catholic girls' school in Michigan.

One evening after graduation Mom answered the phone and the voice on the other end said, "I'm Sister Mary from St. Mary of the Woods and I would like to interview your daughter Warenetta about attending our college." My mom said, "I don't have a daughter, I have a son named Warren."

I never told Mom the story behind that phone call. Every day I would sit in the yearbook office and collect payments from the students who signed up for the yearbook. At that time the yearbook sold for two dollars and the students were allowed to pay fifty cents per quarter. Of course all of these payments had to be recorded on their respective cards. One of Uncle Newt's famous tricks was to come into the annual office, which was adjacent to his classroom, and toss up all the money I had collected that day on the floor. He later had to pick it up.

Every year an Echo queen was chosen. The queen was chosen by the student body and she was allowed to select her own escort. In those days a certain clique dominated the selection of the queen. You might call it high society because they all used their influence and no one outside their clique was ever elected queen. I'm sure that these days there is more equality among the students. Uncle Newt in his desire to have me take part in all the activities picked me up at the house, the evening of the coronation, and took me over to the Echo office where I watched the girls prepare for the procession. After the queen was selected, they all returned to the Echo office. At this point Uncle Newt put the crown on my head. I have the picture in my scrapbook.

The following year after I had graduated Uncle Newt joined the army as a second lieutenant and the yearbook staff decided to dedicate that year's yearbook to Uncle Newt. I was asked to write the dedication which follows:

February 15, 1943
Dear Uncle Newt,

We, your friends, the students of Webster Groves High School, dedicate this book to you, Lieutenant Newton Settle. Because of the many years of our happy companionship, we do not hesitate to call you "Uncle Newt." You dare not mind, Uncle Newt, because some of your nicknames for us will remain in our memory forever. Your laughs, smiles, jokes, and tricks, which were a part of you, made our classwork and annual work more enjoyable. Yes, former annual members, and we of this year's staff, will always remember the surprise parties, which you pulled off for us. At Christmas time Santa Claus used to come to the annual office, decorating the office with a tree and a fireplace and bringing goodies to fill our tummies. Now, we know who played the part of Santa, because Santa didn't visit the annual office this year. Yes, Uncle Newt, we have discovered that you spoiled us and that your high standard is hard for us to meet, since we can't toss any of our jobs at you anymore. From what has been said, you are able to see why we are getting such a big kick out of dedicating this, your yearbook, to you. May God help you to victory, and return you, Uncle Newt, to us.

Sincerely yours,
The Annualites

Forty years later I drove down to Cape Girardeau to visit Uncle Newt. Although he was in his eighties, when he opened the door he said, "Hi, Bozo," which was the name he gave to me when I worked on the yearbook staff.

He was thrilled that I took the time to visit him and I am happy to say that he still had the same friendly smile and warm heart, exactly like Will Rogers. We had a picnic reminiscing about olden times. When I left he gave me a bear hug and told me how happy I had made him.

During my senior year I took business law and Latin American history in place of chemistry. These courses were on the second tract and the interest and drive of the students was noticeably lower than those to which I was accustomed to. However, one of the boys who always laid around in the back row and had no interest in education, turned out to be a financial wizard. This proves that success in life doesn't always depend on the degree of formal education one possesses.

On June 4, 1942, at eight o'clock in the evening, I graduated from Webster High and felt quite satisfied with myself because I knew I had given it everything I had. Out of 266 students there were seventeen honor graduates. I ranked sixteenth in my class and, of course, Mom and Dad were quite proud.

Since I have told you about my classes, I want to give you an overall view of Webster High and the summer activities. During the time I attended Webster High the education system of Webster Groves was ranked one of the highest in the nation. All the teachers were well qualified and very specialized in their field. The man who was the dramatics teacher was named Eugene Wood. Woody produced some outstanding plays, one of which was Thornton Wilder's *Our Town*. I will never forget the narrator who wore a fedora and told about the life in Grover's Corner, as the actors acted out the parts on the stage.

Another one of the special teachers was Ms. Replogle, a thin wiry woman who had a lot of fun managing her choirs. Every year the choir performed the Christmas story including the three wise men and all the other characters. Every spring Ms. Rep produced an outstanding operetta. For all her tireless work one year she was recognized as Webster Groves' Citizen of the Year. Throughout the years we had a weekly assembly, 90 percent of which were educational and very enlightening. Several days before Halloween the police chief of Webster Groves would address the assembly and urge the students to go easy on everybody else's property. The Thanksgiving football game between Webster and Kirkwood has continued throughout the years. In those years the thought of having a gun at the game was simply non-existent. Regretfully, two or three years ago a Kirkwood student brought a gun to the football game and when the gun went off a person was injured.

All through my years at Webster High the education system was not integrated. The blacks had their own grade school and high school, and the thought of integration was the furthest thing from anyone's mind. I must admit that at that time I had very little regard for the African-American race, mainly because that was the way I was raised.

One could argue this point, but all through my high school years every girl wore a dress and every boy wore slacks, shirt and sweater. Long hair and blue jeans were out of the question. In my own opinion the uniformity of dress and hair style contributed to the good behavior of the students. Drugs and guns were never thought of.

All my summers during high school were spent as a volunteer worker in the high school office. J. T. Hixson, a kindly graying man, was principal. He was very easy going except for one day when Mary Marshall, his secretary, threw out by accident the final exams which the teachers had left for the students to make up. It was a hot day in the old town. Mr. Latta, a very intense man, was principal of junior high, and Ms. Ridgeway was his secretary. Over the years I have noticed that many intense people develop mental problems. In his later years, Mr. Latta developed Alzheimer's. The other assistant principal was Joe Verby. For several years he nearly killed himself working on his Ph.D. I never was convinced it was worth all the energy he expended. After receiving his degree Dr. Verby decided that he wanted to learn how the other half lived. Consequently, he took a job at Scullin Steel, firing their furnaces, which turned the ore into steel. Naturally the working conditions were hotter than hell. Dr. Verby would start work at the high school at 8:00 A.M. and leave at 2:00 P.M. for his other job at Scullin Steel Company. After a while you could tell he was really beat up. Dr. Verby died at a relatively early age and I always thought his degree and some of the work contributed to his early demise. It is interesting that in spite of their education both Mr. Hixson and Dr. Verby employed my services after I opened my income tax business.

My main job in the office was to sort the mail, alphabetize various files, etc. At lunch Harry Biederman, one of my classmates who was the receiving clerk at the time, and I, would take our brown bags and go out under the tree at Selma and Lockwood and eat our lunch. One summer Harry had to put graphite in all 1800 locks used on the lockers. He would come to lunch so dirty you wouldn't believe it. It probably took him a week after they were done to get all the graphite off his skin. Harry was one of the honor graduates and after he received his Ph.D. he became the chief economist for the Lockheed Aircraft Company. Harry raised a lovely family and upon his death all of his children wrote eulogies expressing their love and appreciation for having a loving and caring father.

Although I worked every summer, Mom, Dad and I always took a two week vacation. The first summer we explored the Ozarks. The next summer they took me to one of the big paper mills in Kalamazoo, Michigan, from whom my father purchased paper. It was quite a thrill to see the logs turned into pulp and the pulp turned into paper. From Michigan we went to Niagara Falls and stayed at a bed and breakfast. I always wanted to know what they meant by Canadian bacon, so our hostess served that for breakfast. On our way home we visited Deerfield Village where Ford has a model of every Ford car ever built and other interesting collections of antiques.

The next summer Aunt Pearl, accompanied by one of her friends, treated Mom and I to a conducted tour by train and bus that included an overnight stay in Colorado Springs in the famous Broadmore Hotel. The next morning a tour car picked us up and we started out for Pike's Peak. When we left Colorado Springs it was eighty degrees and there was still snow on the top of the peak. The way up was quite exciting because there were no guard rails on the many hairpin curves. We were brought back to Colorado Springs for lunch after which we got back in the tour car and started out for Mount Cheyenne. The Will Rogers' Shrine is built halfway up the mountain and we enjoyed seeing it. The next morning we got back on the train and headed for Salt Lake City. After an overnight stay and tour of Salt Lake City, which included the Mormon Tabernacle, we took another bus and spent a night each at Bryce Canyon, the Grand Canyon and the Zion Canyon. Each canyon was completely different and quite exciting to see. On the way to Bryce Canyon the bus drove through a forest where we saw many deer and other wild animals. We stayed overnight at Bryce and the next morning we got back on the bus and headed for the north rim of Grand Canyon. At the Grand Canyon it was a thrill to eat in the main dining room of the lodge that was built on the edge of the canyon where you could see the sun setting over the canyon. From the Grand Canyon we were taken to Zion Canyon where we spent another night, and the next day we walked through the bottom of Zion Canyon and looked up to the heavens. At Bryce and Grand Canyons you looked down into the canyon itself but at Zion the lodge was at the bottom of the canyon and we looked up to the heavens. Of all the canyons, Bryce impressed me most because of its many rock formations. At each canyon, the college students served the meals and put on a variety show in the evenings. From Zion Canyon we returned to Salt Lake City where we boarded the train back to St. Louis. On the way back the train went through the Royal Gorge and stopped under the bridge that spans the gorge. After being home for just a week Dad took his vacation and Mom, Dad and I started out for Florida. We drove directly to Miami Beach where we stayed three days and toured the city and looked at the wealthy homes in the surrounding communities. We stayed in the Norman Hotel and had a beachfront room on the first floor. All we had to do was open our door, walk down a few steps and we were on the beach. At the time we were there the temperature was ninety-eight degrees in St. Louis and eighty-five degrees at Miami Beach. I enjoyed having the windows open at night and listening to the waves of the ocean. It was wonderful. On the way home we stopped at Silver Springs where we could see the fish from a glass-bottomed boat. We also visited Cypress Gardens and the Bach Singing

Tower. Nowadays, Disney World and Epcot Center are located nearby. At that time no one imagined that a variety of mechanical entertainment and scientific inventions would ever be created, much less displayed. From there we headed home through the Smoky Mountains. It was a wonderful way to spend the four weeks before I started my senior year at Webster High School.

After my senior year, the question of where I was going to college was settled for me. My faith in Christian Science was shattered after I was successfully mainstreamed with 1800 students at Webster High and they would not let me in Principia with 300 students. Since Westminster College was a small Presbyterian school I was told that was where I was going. Because of the war, gasoline was rationed and consequently I never saw the school or met any of the faculty or even inspected the place where I was going to live. All of these arrangements were made for me by Mr. Keel, a field representative of Westminster College. If I had been shown my living and dining facilities I probably would never have gone to Fulton, Missouri.

3
My College Years

On a Sunday morning in September of 1942, Mom, Dad and I picked up Charles Bush, the student Mr. Keel had arranged for me to live with at the last minute. He lived with his father and his mother had either died or was divorced. It was the first time I met the lad and one might say "we were the odd couple." We drove up Highway 40 to Kingdom City and then went nine miles south to Fulton, Missouri, the county seat of Calloway County. As is customary with all county seats, the courthouse was in the main square surrounded by all types of stores. We went directly to the house which was to be my future home away from home. The address was 221 West Sixth Street, which jogged. My house was on the jog, next to an empty lot. The next step was to meet my landlady, Lida Harrison, a kindly elderly woman. She showed Charles and me up to our upstairs room. I had the main room and my roommate had a smaller room off to the side. It was fortunate that there was a door between the rooms because no matter how cold it was he slept with the windows wide open. Charles had many odd habits and was not much of a student. The furniture in my room consisted of a double bed, study table and chair. In the other room on the same floor was a middle-aged woman of low mentality and she cooked in her room and pined over the fact that her son was in the service. The bathroom consisted of a wash basin, toilet and old-fashioned bathtub with claw feet. It was very difficult to see Mom and Dad leave but I put up a brave front.

In the early evening, Charles and I walked down to the Woolery Cafe where I ate lunch and supper all the time while I was in Fulton. My usual lunch consisted of a pork loin sandwich and a glass of milk. It was strictly a country cafe. For dinner, along with your entree you had your choice of three side dishes out of a list of ten. Mr. Woolery was a stout bald-headed man and his two daughters served as waitresses. He sold five-dollar tickets for four dollars and fifty cents numbered with various amounts around the edge. After every meal he would punch the correct amount from your ticket. In the fall of the year when we got back to our rooming house, there was a flock of grackles that landed on the lot every evening and made an unbelievable racket.

The next morning I walked the two blocks to the campus and then up one more hill to the main building, where I enrolled as a freshman. I was given the customary blue beanie which all freshmen were required to wear. Somehow I lost my beanie and when I put a note on the bulletin board to that effect the only response was "too bad."

My courses, which were pre-arranged for me, consisted of:

English I, taught by a very young professor, Mr. Gordon. In reality the course was simply a review of all the grammar I had already learned in high school. In retrospect, I can't understand why we were never requested to write an essay or story.

Old Testament History, taught by an elderly gentlemen, Mr. McQueen, whose false teeth were about ready to fall out when he spoke. Since he spent the whole semester covering the book of Genesis, I often wondered how many years I would have to stay there to cover the whole Old Testament.

Personal Hygiene was an interesting course concerning the human body. It was taught by the basketball coach, Coach Kimball, who was one of the few teachers who showed me a little warmth. One icy morning when I split my knee open after a fall he was kind enough to stop class and bandage my knee.

French was taught by a typical young Frenchman, whose name was Mr. Dahl. Regardless of the weather he rode his bicycle to school and wore a beret. I had French every morning at 8:00 A.M. and walked to class in the complete darkness since we were on war time. Often the moon and stars were still shining.

Algebra II was taught by the aging dean, George B. Sweazey. This was the only course that gave me a little trouble because advanced math was not my strong subject.

Latin Derivatives was taught by a plump young professor, Dr. Skiles. After four years of Latin it was a snap. All the classes were held in the morning and many of the professors, along with the students, went down the hill at noon. Many drove cars and in spite of all kinds of weather, I was only offered a ride once to the Woolery's Cafe, which was six blocks away.

Every afternoon I spent pouring over my subjects and outlined whatever I could. I would stop to go down to Woolery's again for my supper and then come back to study some more until bedtime. Naturally, being away from home for the first time I had the worst case of homesickness that anyone could have. Now in retrospect, I only wonder why my parents didn't take a little money from the trust that Aunt Tillie left me to have a phone installed in my room. It would have been a great help and really given me a lot of joy. At this time I should mention that Mrs. Harrison brought me up a bowl of peaches, orange juice and milk every morning for breakfast. Now I think how nice it would have been if I could have gone down to her kitchen and had a little conversation with her before going to class. I always mailed Mrs. Harrison a Christmas card and years later her daughter phoned me from Springfield to tell me how much Mrs. Harrison had enjoyed my annual Christmas card.

The boys' dormitory was 200 feet from the main classroom building. The president's residence was between the two buildings. Across the street from the president's residence was the chapel which housed the library in its basement. Unfortunately, I was not allowed to live in the boys' dormitory because several years before my appearance on the horizon, they had a similar cerebral palsy person. He must have been one unbelievable hell raiser. Without even seeing me or getting any references they made the arbitrary decision that I was unfit to live in the boys' dorm; but they were damn glad to take my money.

Now that I look back on the situation I regret that I was so conscientious in my studies. I feel that if I had spent a little time hanging around the boys' dorm and some of the fraternity houses I could have made friends with a few of my classmates and avoided some of my homesickness. Since it was in the middle of the war we often had blackouts and I remember lying in my bed in complete darkness. Another depressing incident I saw while I was eating lunch in Woolery's one rainy afternoon was seeing thirty or forty young men leaving for the service while their families were weeping. All these conditions did not contribute to the happiness of a young freshman away from home for the first time. In spite of all these obstacles I would like to list my final report card.

> English I—95
> Old Testament History—90
> Personal Hygiene—91
> French I—96
> Algebra II—88
> Latin Derivatives—96

The dean noted on the bottom of the report card, "An excellent record." In spite of all my grades no attempt was made to accommodate my needs. Consequently, I packed my bag and came home.

Since it is now fifty years later I want to assure my readers that Westminster College would not treat me in the same manner. All colleges are now eager to adapt to the needs of the handicapped. Today Westminster is a fine coed college and exchanges classes with William Woods College, which was an exclusive girls' college when I attended Westminster. Westminster has graduated many prominent people. I regret I could not have finished my four years there because I would have loved to have been there when Churchill made his famous Iron Curtain address, or been an alumni when Gorbachev spoke there recently.

After I came home from Westminster College in April 1943, I wrote the following essay because I had idle time and writing was one of my forte:

From a Post-graduate to a Graduating Senior

> Graduating seniors, you know how to divide, multiply and subtract. You probably have been taught the history

of the world, many scientific principles, and many other necessities of life; but the backbone of our civilized universe, namely, the fraternal association with other human beings, has been neglected or shied away from by your instructors. Probably you have had the opportunity or have taken time to ponder over the traits, manners, and reactions of persons with whom you come in contact daily. When Bill crabs with Joe, the first thought you have nis that Bill is in a bad mood. That word "mood" has freed the conscience of more individuals than God has freed by putting people to rest. Why should we blame our unprincipled habits on that much abused term, "mood," when we could eliminate moods by thinking before we talk, and before we make one of our kin unhappy without reason. Since moods are merely expressions of feeling, why not smile away your pain and maltreatment, instead of causing other people to be down-pressed by your thoughtless fussing. If you carry out this suggestion, you'll have to grit your teeth severely the first time; but after each succeeding episode, your grit will become less painful, until finally your mind and body will harmonize into an enchanting melody, which, of course, never contains one sour note.

Your mind, soul, and physical body are much like a house, which is beaten and shattered by winds, cleaned and polished by rains, and made more endurable by the work and patience of skilled hands. Having attended a credible high school for four years, you are justified in thinking that the foundation of your house is firm and unbreakable. Yes, in a certain sense you are right in your assumption; but are you sure that it can withstand a violent wind or a drenching rain? Contrary to your beliefs, your lives have been sheltered by your parents, teachers and companions. If a storm hits you in the form of a bloody nose, you always have had your parents to give you assurance and aid; or if you shot someone with a water gun there was almost always somebody present to curb your natural streak of devilishment, which is usually embedded in all mankind. In fact, I dare say that nary a one of you have made an important decision without consulting one or more of your trustworthy friends. But, whether in college, in a defense plant, or on a blistering hot battlefield, the day will come when you can't confide an ultimate decision in your chum or pal. What are you going to do? Will you let your sturdy feet fling you down the path of least resistance, or will you let your immortal mind be the master of your corporeal foundation? By taking the hardest path when two pathways are available, you will in the future be able to walk the straight and narrow path and behold the tiny ray of guiding light, which is always present. For animals who have limited reasoning power, God sees to it that certain of his creatures take the hardest path by having them store away food when it is plentiful. Are you not going to develop this instinct, which is sprouting in all persons your age, and prove that you are on a higher level than lower classes of animals?

The bones and flesh of your body correspond to the bricks and walls of a house. No matter how frail the walls of a house are, they will invariably endure the toughest beating if the walls are built on a solid foundation. The same fact holds true concerning the human body. If you have a good moral support, the size and shape of your mortal body need not be given a thought, since it is only one among a billion other oddities. Since a dwelling could not stand without beams, rafters, and other supports, your body cannot stand without integrity, perseverance, and a certain amount of education. If you have the privilege of attending college, you should put the desire to learn first and to have a good time with acquaintances second. In college over half of the students seek pleasure before education. Most of these young people rejoice over the fact that their parents are not there to advise and guide them. If this is your reaction why not obtain the education of getting along with your parents before stumbling blindly out into the world-pool of life. Just because you get As in school and are popular with the gang is no reason that you should fail to respect your mother and heed her suggestions or notice the poor students who long for your help and friendship. Although a fellow student might appear to be slow in developing his intelligence, you better pass some kind words along to him, because later in life when you go to him for advice or for a job, he'll recall how you have treated him. However, this type of person will probably never mention how you treated him in his school days, so why not handle everyone with equality from now on and play the game of life fairly and squarely. Therefore, you can perceive the fact that new acquaintances at college are lasting contacts, and are nearly as significant as an education, so long as you can put a stopwatch on your social whirl. Two typical examples will illustrate this point. Once, an old friend, who ranked first in his graduating high school class, and is not making As in college, greeted his former school mate cordially, asked him a few questions, and then stared blankly for an hour while the former made the conversation. He connected everything with scientific facts and ancient mythology, disrespecting human life and the joys of living. When he was persuaded to walk to the bus, he insisted on taking a book along, so that his time would not be wasted on his return trip. This person is losing the joy of being an American by neglecting to observe other Americans, to talk with them and to mingle with them. Even if he has a chance of becoming an outstanding historian, he will probably be a drudge to his students and lose their respect, since he will not understand their ways and means of expression. On the other hand, several capable people have gone to college and have become involved in so many activities, that they couldn't devote the proper amount of time to any one thing. The consequences were the failure to do any job well, and the unfair degrading of their ego. People who attend college or enter the business world should follow the middle path. This road consists of choosing one occupation and one hobby and performing both of these with continued perseverance and integrity. If any person is so talented that he is capable of handling and excelling in more than two things satisfactorily he should have the opportunity to blossom out fully. Remember, a house with a firm base does not require so many beams and supports. If you have made a failure of your education thus far, don't fret over it. Instead rely on your natural foundation—integrity and perseverance—which, of course if used correctly, are always a means of reaching the top. In other words, the man who applies a little integrity and constantly sticks to his job will always progress regardless of his past history.

Your brain is the roof of your abode, and its strength to keep out the cold thoughts, the raging furies, the red hot angers, the pouring torments, and the flashing moods of life hinges upon its dilation. A brain trained in civil rights and decencies will shut out all of the malefactors of life, keeping the body cool and even-tempered. Nevertheless, most human brains are equipped with intake valves through which drenching agonies pour, and out-take valves through which fighting red rays shoot forth. It is highly essential that you should spend time on the insulation of your roof, since it is really your protective covering against the outside beatings of life. Many people resemble a certain widow whose son was in the armed forces. Since her income was meager and her education scant, she thought that the whole world was down on her. One month when her government paycheck arrived late, her phone happened to be out of order. Instantly, she bellowed that her phone had been disconnected because of her failure to pay the bill promptly. This helpless soul had many openings in her flimsily constructed roof, the largest of which was the loophole labeled "faith in life." If you are going to pattern yourself after the pitiful person just mentioned, you are doomed to live a wretched and fearful life. No one was ever born a thief, but the treatment received during his life molded his character in the wrong direction. When you see someone going downhill, don't punish him severely; instead, correct his viewpoints and try your level best to give him a faith in life and God that will carry him over all the rocky bumps in the track of success. Many people have faith in life while everything is going smoothly for them; but let them step on one sharp pebble, and their golden trust is shattered beyond repair. When you pass into the outer world, why don't you pick out the thorns as they prick your vulnerable soul and have the confidence in life to know that if you succeed in extracting the core of the thorn, you will never be menaced by the same thing again.

The extermination of life's thorns might be such a painful process that tears cannot be restrained. Don't be ashamed to weep, because it is one of the most beautiful things in life. When homes become coated with the dust of the earth, God sends rain to wash this foreign matter away. The All-Powerful performs the same service for human beings. When their mind is troubled and when their heart is sad, He sometimes sends water to wash away the dirt and grime from their windows. After the water evaporates or is dried up, you view offenses with an altogether different attitude and are willing to forgive and become cheerful again. However, after an injustice has been brought upon some persons, they are not willing to let their sorrow flow away in tears. Instead, these misunderstanding souls become indignant—hot and ruffled—and seek revenge rather than a peaceful settlement. A typical example occurs when Jane doesn't invite Lois to a party, since Jane doesn't think that Lois would mix freely with the crowd. Not attempting to perceive the good thought behind the act of Jane's, Lois will seek revenge by high-hatting Jane at their next meeting, and before long a vicious circle of nasty remarks is progressing with accelerated speed. Why seek revenge? Look at the world today. Yes, a horrible battle is being fought: lives are being lost, minds are being contaminated, and sorrows and griefs, and more important, bitter pains are being endured. Revenge! Revenge is the cause of our present strife. Just because two or three greedy minds are not willing to be satisfied with their vast resources and so-called injustices, they are revenging the world with a barbarous and uncivilized war. In the future let nature take care of our grievances and bury your hate and revenge in the blessed tears of Mother Nature.

Your house, being properly built, possesses a front and back door. Of course, your ears do not swing on hinges; but they have the power of letting certain things in and keeping other things out. If you have sturdy, close-fitting doors, only the righteous thoughts will enter into your palace. But, if you allow your doors to warp and buckle, misconstructed words will enter, devastating your opinion of good friends and true facts. Are you going to be fickle and believe idle gossip along with proven data, or will you weather-strip your portals sifting out the good from the bad, the true from the false and the encouraging from the disheartening? As you enter your next span of life, many uplifting thoughts and many degrading words will pierce your trap door. Won't you please put a plumb bob on your two doors so that you can carefully weigh everything which you hear? By doing this, you can make a wholesome judgment on each problem which confronts you and keep a lot of grief and misery out of the world.

Graduating seniors, you are probably asking yourselves, "Who in the devil is this writer? Does he think he is better than we are? What right have we to respect his advice?" Fellow students, all the answers are No. He is proud that he is an ordinary mortal man with his own faults. If he were perfect, life would be a bore to him. He would not be able to profit by any interesting experiences, or to strive for improvement. Since he is no better than you are, you shouldn't respect his advice. He merely is attempting to toss out some thoughts for you to ponder over, and some problems which have faced him. Please be open-minded and consider the author of this as just one more person who is struggling with everyone else in the world-pool of life.

I would particularly like to emphasize the following ideas: If you go to work, go to the army, or attend school, discouraging orders will be given to you. No matter what they are, do them with a smile and make everyone around you as cheerful as you can. If you have a friend at work when you are attending college, and if you should both be called to serve in the armed services, don't try to decide who is making the biggest sacrifice. Simply answer the call and serve to the best of your ability, encouraging your friend unceasingly. If you have seen your old playmates, new friends, and your favorite teacher join the army, navy or the marines while you remain on the home front, don't fret about it. You can do your duty by writing encouraging letters to them, giving them laughs and relating the happenings that are occurring on their old stamping grounds. It means a lot to hear from a friend when you are away.

As a final suggestion I would like to quote a passage taken from the *Reader's Digest*. "Everyone has a wonderful opportunity to make a success of his life, if he has a reasonable intelligence, ambition, and the willingness to do hard work."

From January to June of 1943 I did odd jobs at Webster High School. That summer I took English II at Washington University to complete my Freshmen English. It was a six-week course and I made a B. Then they had a five-week six-day term and one of the advisors enrolled me in English Literature I and English Literature II. English Literature I was from 7:30 to 9:30 A.M. and English Literature II was from 10:00 to 12:00 noon. I rode over to the university in the cool of the morning with a neighbor, Mr. Skinner, who worked in the area. After my 12:00 noon class I took the bus home in the beastly heat of a typical St. Louis summer. This was as near as any suicidal period I ever experienced. The two professors must have taken pity on me and I got Cs. I was never so thankful to get away from that drudgery. In the winter of 1943 I took a beginning psychology course at Washington University. All the classes at the university were simply too large for me and I felt like a number. Consequently in the spring of 1944, I decided to forget about education and look for a job. I went to the vocational rehabilitation office and was interviewed by J. I. MacDoniels, a truly dedicated individual. After he gave me an IQ test on which I scored 132, he said I was going to college. I replied "Okay Mister, you find me a college where I can live in the dorm and I will go."

Fortunately, he knew of Culver-Stockton College and one warm April day he rode up with Mom, Dad and me. I was interviewed by the professor of education, who was acting as an admissions counselor. He had an especially large jowl and all the students called him "hog jowl." When Dr. Knapp saw my grades from Westminster and asked me a few questions he said, "We will be happy to have you and you can start this summer's trimester." They already had one cerebral palsy person as a student and he was doing fairly well.

About the third week of May, Mom and Dad drove me up to Culver-Stockton with all the necessary clothes for the summer.

Canton is a small river town on the Mississippi River and the college is its main industry. The college is five blocks from the main street. The four main cross streets (Washington, Lewis, Clark and College) are lined with many trees and small well-kept houses. The town's main business district consisted of the usual enterprises of a small town, including the picture show which charged twenty-five cents and a one-man barber shop who charged thirty-five cents for a haircut. The barber's name was Matt and he was as slow as a tortoise. Of course the town also had a small county bank known as the Canton State Bank and a small public library. On the other side of Main Street was the one and only manufacturing plant and the local tavern which was strictly off-limits to the students. At one end of Main Street was the Canton Hotel, which, at that time, was used by many businessmen and was an ideal place to spend the night. It had a small dining room adjacent to a tiny lobby. In the summer, chairs were put out on the side of the hotel where the customers could sit in the cool of the evening.

I met the housemother, Mabel Yaeger, who made me feel at home from the very start. In order to make things easier for me they put me in a room directly opposite the bathroom, which I regretted because it was a dreadfully hot summer and all the other rooms were able to open their doors on the other side of the hall and get a breeze through their rooms while I sweltered. That first Sunday evening Mrs. Yaeger made us peanut butter sandwiches since the cook was not hired until the following morning. The young boy in the room next to me was Charles W. Schaeffer. I went in and sat with him for a few minutes. We both were rather lonely and didn't know what the future held for us. Chuck was a tall, lanky small-town boy fresh out of high school. His home was in Palmyramo, which is twenty-five miles from Canton. His father was a blacksmith and our backgrounds were very different. However, we became good friends and have remained so for over fifty years.

We walked from Wood Hall, the boys' dorm, past five small cottages, which served as faculty residences, up to Henderson Hall, which was the girls' dorm. The entire summer school student body sat on the steps in preparation for a vesper service. From the steps one could see over the town of Canton and view the Mississippi River. The vesper service was led by Dr. John Alexander. He was a huge man with small beady eyes and a warm smile. In time to come I enjoyed his courses in religion, philosophy, and ethics. As I became familiar with him I spent quite a few Saturday evenings with him and his wife in their apartment, which I couldn't do at Westminster. I think they enjoyed my visits because Dr. Alexander's wife was handicapped. After the vesper service I returned to Wood Hall which served as my home for the next two years.

The next morning I went up to the gymnasium, which was the only other building on campus besides the administration building, to enroll as a sophomore. The fee for the semester's tuition was $125 plus $125 for room and board. The same fee nowadays is about $6,500.

Tuesday morning I eagerly started my classes and since the history professor wasn't hired until the fall semester, Rev. Roy Blalock filled in and taught me my first semester of U.S. History. Besides that course I had him for two psychology courses and in all three courses he gave me a C+. (When I came to graduation I had a 91.87 average. Ninety-two was required for cum laude. Roy said to me "Slick, you probably earned a B in all those courses but I didn't want to give you too much encouragement.") Shouldn't that be called "discouragement." Those were the only Cs I ever received at Culver-Stockton. My other courses were: Human Geography taught by Dean Hopkins. He was on his last legs and passed away that December. He always had a twinkle in his eye and when he laughed he slapped his feet together. Another course was Trigonometry, taught by Mrs. Cook, a Christian Scientist. My best course, which I am saving for the last, was Principles of Economics, taught by Joe Hootman, under whom I took many future courses. Mr. Hootman was a laid-back individual. He always taught his courses by sitting in a chair with his elbow leaning on the arm of the chair and his chin resting in his hand. It was so hot that summer and since there were only eight students in the class, Mr. Hootman had nine desks moved out into the quadrangle and we held class under a shady tree. Since it was during the war, we did three semesters' work in a year, which was called trimesters; consequently we had classes on Saturdays. The first Saturday was a Monday, the second Saturday was Tuesday, and so on, until all three weeks were taken care of. In hot weather those Saturday afternoon classes were for the birds.

During that summer there were so few students that both the girls and the boys ate at the Wood Hall dining room, which was in the basement of the boys' dorm. About three weeks into the summer trimester, the college played host to a church conference. The young boys used the upstairs rooms of the boys' dorm and the young girls did the same thing in the girls' dorm. The basement of the girls' dorm was ground level and it contained the laundry room. At night the young girls would wash out their underclothes and go to bed. One evening some of the boys, I don't know who, put their hands through the windows and snatched some of the undergarments. The next morning they were found streaming in the breeze on top of the flagpole in the quadrangle. Reverend Blalock was quite disturbed and really chewed the boys out.

We were about four weeks into the summer trimester when two college students, who were officers of the local chapter of the Lambda Chi Alpha fraternity, came to see me in my room to ask me some questions. They were not attending summer school and were driving a vending route when they took a few minutes off to see what kind of guy I was. One thing in my favor was that Dwain Nichols, who was one of the officers, had a deaf and dumb brother who was attending a school in Fulton; therefore, he made no bones about my handicap, and in about a week I was asked to join the fraternity. About a week later I came down for supper in a new white California suit. The president of the fraternity said, "Boy, you look slick." And from then on, all through my life, I was known as Slick.

A few weeks later Robert Lemon, the president of the fraternity, along with his girlfriend and another couple, went over to an island in the Mississippi for a picnic and went wading in the river. He got caught in the undertow and drowned. Of course it was a sad day and all the fraternity members and pledges attended his funeral in Palmyra, Missouri. I grew to love Palmyra because it was the home of Chuck Schaeffer, who became my lifelong friend.

During the fall trimester of 1944, I took several history courses and American literature, plus accounting. I took the American lit course since I had to wait for Economics II to be taught during the spring trimester. The literature course was taught by Mrs. Ada Roberts whose room was on the second floor of the administration building and in the winter time I could see the Mark Twain Zephyr coming down from Iowa heading toward my home in St. Louis. Mrs. Roberts taught at Culver for many many years and the boys affectionately referred to her as "Ada Beta." Upon her death, a new concourse up the hill to the college was named in her honor, and a stone entrance bears her name. Upon her retirement her former students were requested to write a tribute to her. I herewith submit my thoughts about her.

September 25, 1948
Dear Mrs. Roberts,

Although most people believe that I attended Culver-Stockton when general conditions on the campus were at low ebb, I consider just the opposite to be true. At no other time in the history of our alma mater were the classes as small as they were during the middle period of the Second World War. Consequently, being a student at this time, I was given the privilege of knowing, understanding, and evaluating the goals of each of my instructors better than many students who graduated before or since those war-torn years. Because of this close contact with you, not only as a teacher, but as a friend, I feel proficiently qualified to make the following remarks in celebration of your silver anniversary as a C-S professor.

Most professors like to be remembered for their skill in rattling off dates, names and definitions, which the average student cheerfully forgets in a year or two. I think you will be pleased to know that I don't remember you in this light. Whenever I think of Mrs. Roberts, nouns, verbs, poems, or verse does not dominate my thinking. Rather I invariably recall your enthusiasm, your interest in the problems of your struggling, struggling students, and most notably your interpretation of the material at hand.

If anyone has ever seen you walk, or heard you talk, they'll never in the world doubt your enthusiasm. Unlike many professors, your inspiration is not limited to your subject but rather it includes every aspect of college life. May you never lose this rare sense of balance, because to me, appreciating the stillness of a Canton snowstorm is equally as important as reading Emerson's "The Snowstorm," or experiencing the oncoming of spring to the Hill is just as revealing as Richard Hovey's "Spring."

Your recent appointment to Dean of Women proves that the college administrators recognized your interests and abilities in helping students. Because of a little word of encouragement, patience in explaining things, which many people would consider elementary, and a frequent smile, you have saved many promising students from discouragement and despair. May you continue to broaden your understanding of young America and profit by your continuing experiences—a rare and admirable trait. By reading the textbook you use in Freshmen English, by enjoying one semester of American Literature under your guidance, and by frequent conversations with you, I am convinced that you have a unique technique of interpretation. America is your home and you'll argue forever that our way is more wholesome over the long run than socialism, fascism or communism. God grant that we may have more teachers of youth, who do not give facts alone, but instead reveal the hidden opportunities of America through his subject matter and his philosophy of life.

It is my sincere wish that the future hold many more profitable years for you and your students on the Hill. May you continue to be inspired by the "Star" at Christmas, by the flowing "Mississippi," and by everything on campus which you cherish.

Sincerely,
Warren E. Gerlach, Class of '46

At the end of the trimester we had to close a complete

set of books in my accounting course. It was quite a task to do on the typewriter but I completed it without a mistake.

At the beginning of the spring trimester 1945, my accounting professor announced that we had to close another set of books for practice and my U.S. History professor announced that we had to learn the names of all the Civil War generals and know whether they were for the North or South. Also, all during my college years I spent hours and hours every evening outlining the chapters of every textbook I had. Early in the trimester one Saturday afternoon I started to cry. The housemother seemed to know it was a small nervous breakdown and called my parents. They immediately drove up and took me home late Saturday night. I spent Sunday at home and they put me back on the train on Monday morning and I was back in school Tuesday morning. Reverend Blalock immediately contacted me and said "Slick, please stop outlining your books. You are smart enough to pass without doing all that work." But, being a stubborn Dutchman, I continued my outlines. Then Joe Hootman contacted me and said that since I had done a perfect job in closing my first set of books he would excuse me from the second set. That was the only break I ever received.

The other two interesting courses that trimester were Sociology, taught by Dr. Lacey Lee Leftwich, and U.S. History, taught by Dr. Ford Messamore. Lacey Lee was a very unconventional professor. He didn't teach by the book. He wanted his students to be aware of their environment and continually preached interaction and conditioning as an important part of the development of character. Once he gave a test on the subject covered by the book. Everyone did so well he disregarded the test grade. One day I'll never forget my friend, Nick, was sitting in the back row of the sociology course and Lacey asked him a question. He answered, "My mother married her brother but I'm okay." Of course, the class howled. Lacey had his pets and fortunately I was one. I knew exactly what he wanted us to do on his tests and I fed it to him full force. Consequently, he always gave me an A. I spent many Saturday nights with him and his wife arguing different points of view. They had lost their only son at an early age and I think they used me as a substitute.

Dr. Ford Messamore always wore a black suit, black tie and a white shirt regardless of the temperature. He had clammy white skin and to me appeared half dead. He drove an ancient Ford and he never socialized with the other professors. I always wondered what his wife looked like. Although Reverend Blalock gave me a C+ in U.S. History I, Dr. Messamore gave me an A in U.S. History II. I kind of agree with Reverend Blalock that I probably earned at least a B. Later on I took a year of political science from Dr. Messamore. Every two weeks he would give an objective test with 100 questions. Each student had his own number and the scores were posted on the bulletin board. Without failure I always had the highest score and consequently got an A. Fortunately I had a good memory and I could forget the statistics as quickly as I could learn them. Dr. Messamore's two pet sayings were, "Who said what America needs is a good five-cent cigar?"—the answer was John Marshall who ran for vice president with Woodrow Wilson. His other stickler was, "The House of Representatives always would have 435 Representatives."

After sweltering in Room 17 my first summer I used my charm and personality to get the southeast corner room in Wood Hall. This was my hangout for the next two years and I loved that room. Chuck and his roommate, Don Stukenbroeker, moved next door. Mom and Dad sent up an easy chair with a straw carpet for the floor. Of course all the students accused me of being a plutocrat. However, they were mighty happy to invade my room every time I received my laundry box from home. They knew it always contained a tin box of Toll House cookies, and they devoured them quickly. Can you believe in those days I used to mail my laundry box home for thirty-five cents?

Some of the students in the dorm were quite interesting. One was Johan Sverdrup, the son of Gen. Leif Sverdrup, who was a famous engineer in World War II. We also had two other cerebral palsy students besides myself. Rayford Lindsey West was there a year before I was, but he stayed out for the summer trimester. Before I came the students catered to his whims and whams and treated him with kid gloves. His parents were Presbyterians but he attended a Catholic School in Palmyra, Missouri. Those sisters really did a snow job on him because every night he would go to bed at nine o'clock and get up at six o'clock in the morning to say his beads. One evening he was eating supper at my table and one of the boys said, "Notre Dame sure has a lousy football team this year." And just because it was a Catholic school, Rayford got mad as a wet hen. Then once in a while you would come in late for dinner. The students would heckle you; and when they heckled him, he got red as a fire cracker. When the same thing happened to me, I would say, "You should have seen her, she was beautiful." When Rayford was out in a group and came to a door he would insist on opening the door for everybody. While on the other hand I said, "Thank you very much," and walked in. Since the boys could wrestle with me and since I got in on all the bull sessions late at night, the boys dropped Rayford like a hot potato. In addition, Rayford was a rabid Republican and he couldn't tolerate any other person's viewpoint. To top it off Rayford wanted to become a chemist. Of all the asinine ideas—can you imagine anybody with a withered arm trying to become a chemist. Consequently, he dropped out in January and ended up being in charge of the Palmyra, Missouri, library. Every afternoon for forty dollars a month he just sat there and checked in a few books every day. Every time I drove up to Culver-Stockton I would stop by and take him out to supper, which was a real treat for him. All through his life he wore a shirt and tie and never varied his dress.

The other cerebral palsy boy was James Simmons, who was a direct opposite of Rayford. He wanted everybody to do everything for him and was a whiner from the word go. He only lasted one semester. I stayed in the middle of the road and flew through college with flying colors.

May I point out how important it is for everyone, especially a cerebral palsy person, to be a moderate and not be a radical, conservative or liberal. It is important for everyone to see the other person's point of view. You do not have to agree with them, but you should not show your anger concerning their beliefs.

Many of the students that semester were what I would call marginal students. Of course, it was during the war and the college accepted almost any living male that could read. Many of the students only lasted a year at the most and the majority would have been much better off in a vocational school.

There was a lot of ice and snow at the beginning of the spring trimester in 1945. We were still on war time and often the moon was still up when we went to our 8 A.M. class. Unlike Westminster, I had fraternity brothers to get on either side of me and slide me up the hill. When we crossed in front of the girls' dorm and headed toward the administration building where most of my classes were held, the cold wind blew with a bitter chill. My friend, Nick, would say, "Slick, it's colder than a nun's tit in the Klondike."

As the weather warmed up I suppose some of my juices started to flow and I finally got up nerve enough to ask a coed for a date. She immediately accepted and Charlotte Wildman and I went out almost every Wednesday, Saturday and Sunday nights, which were date nights. I think one reason for Charlotte's acceptance of my invitation was the fact that she grew up in Palmyra and attended high school with Rayford West who also was cerebral palsied. Also I had a much better personality and I didn't go around kicking chins like Rayford did. Otherwise, the girls were not allowed to be out after 8 P.M. Even on date nights Charlotte had to be in by 10:30. Our ordinary date consisted of going to the local picture show (which is now closed) and on to the Grand Leader Drug Store where we sat in one of the rear booths and had a "sand storm." For the uninformed person, a sand storm consisted of chocolate ice cream covered with malt. In the spring of the year, while it was still light, Charlotte and I walked down the 100 steps from the college campus into town. The steps were the beginning of Lewis Street which was lined with trees and small well-kept houses. Main Street was five blocks from the campus and it was the main drag of Canton. At that time Highway 61 was part of Main Street. A few years ago they built Highway 61 on the outer rim of Canton, which has dramatically turned Canton into a more peaceful town. In my college days the Canton Hotel was a favorite stopping place for salesmen. It was a very clean hotel with a dining room on the side. Once in a while Charlotte and I would get enough energy to walk five more blocks down to the old Mississippi River. Even though Charlotte and I dated for a year and a half, I never held her hand or made a pass (like a dumb fool). Because of my cerebral palsy I never wanted to make a spectacle of myself and, unfortunately, I was a perfect gentlemen at all times. One night when Charlotte and I returned to campus Charlotte started to wrestle with me. Now I know she must have wanted a kiss or a little loving but at that time I was too naive and too interested in my studies to worry about such things. (I urge parents of other cerebral palsy children to understand that they have the same needs as other teenagers. The parents should advise them that a small pat on a girl's arm or small smack on a girl's cheek is not a cardinal sin.)

The end of World War II was in sight and I was getting damn sick and tired of going to school six days a week. Consequently, I put up a petition on the bulletin board urging that the college go back on a two-semester year. I was the first one to sign it and the petition only remained on the bulletin board about one day. I thought some student had ripped it down and I paid no more attention to it. However, at our next weekly chapel service, President William H. MacDonald, opened his weekly address by saying, "Ladies and gentlemen, I want it firmly understood that whenever you have an idea, my office door is always open, but please never write a petition. I despise them." In the middle of his address he repeated his opening statement, and then at the end of his address he repeated it for the third time. About that time I was about ready to crawl under my seat.

When I got back to the dorm I decided to take the bull by the horns and called up the president's secretary and asked her when I could have an appointment to see the president. She told me, "Three o'clock this afternoon would be fine, Mr. Gerlach." Of course, I wanted to put my best foot forward so I dressed with shirt, tie and coat, and hesitantly went up to face the music. I was shown into the president's office and was asked to take a seat. Immediately, the president told me about all the nice things he had been hearing about me. What a fine student I was and how proud he was of me. Finally, he got around to asking me what I wanted to see him about.

I said, "Come on now, don't you really know?"

"I really don't," he said.

I said, "Didn't you read the first name on the petition?"

He said, "No, I just threw the damn thing away."

I replied, "I happen to be the guy that wrote the petition."

At this point he roared back in his chair with laughter. When I left the office he gave me a picture of himself which I still have, and on the picture, he wrote, "With High Regard," and signed his name. Before I left I said "I thought you would rather read three hundred signatures rather than interview three hundred students."

Instead of going down 100 steps into town, there was a path from the boys' dorm down to Lewis Street. The dorm was at a much lower level than the rest of the campus. The path was not too steep. One Saturday night as I was walking down the path I met two boys coming up from town. They had a bottle of wine and said, "Come on, Slick, have a sip of wine." I took out my straw that I always used for drinking, took a sip of wine and went on downtown for my ice cream. Afterwards, I returned to the dorm, had a few words with Mother Yaeger, and went to bed. Unfortunately, some of the boys drank too much that night and went up to the band room and removed all the instruments and serenaded the music professor at 1 A.M. For some reason, Professor Pierce did not appreciate the interruption. Consequently, when we ate lunch Monday, the dean entered the room and said, "I want to see everybody that was in on the escapade Saturday night in the recreation room," which was in the basement of the boys' dorm. Since I was not involved in any way I went on my merry way. However, one or two of the boys were on the verge of being expelled from college. They said, "You can't throw us out, even Slick had a sip of wine." The outcome was that everyone involved in the incident was confined to campus for the rest of the semester. But everybody said because of Mom and Dad's influence I was not campused. Even so, the word got around that I had a drink and I took a lot of razzing. Since the boys were not allowed to go to town, I guess I rather aggravated the administration, but I did a lot of shopping for the boys. The restriction lasted so long that Matt, the barber, came up on his afternoon off and cut hair in the boys' washroom. The president was known to imbibe now and them. He lifted the restriction after a few weeks.

One more memorable moment of my spring semester was one afternoon in April. I had just returned to my room from taking my daily shower and was putting on my shirt and tie, which was required for dinner every evening, when the announcer on the radio said, "President Roosevelt had died of a cerebral hemorrhage while swimming at Warm Springs, Georgia." The commentator said that Harry S. Truman was now president of the

United States. Everyone wondered how a man without a formal education who used to run a dry goods store and was affiliated with the Pendergast Gang in Kansas City could ever be an acceptable president. However, I read his biography a few years ago and I found him to be a most remarkable and capable president. He accepted all of his responsibilities and on his desk he had the sign, THE BUCK STOPS HERE. However, his wife, Bessie, had a hard time enjoying the social life of Washington and spent much of her time in Independence, Missouri, their home town.

At the end of the semester the college sent my report card home, and I had earned three As and three Bs. My dad wrote me a letter and said, "Why didn't you make all As." Since my dad and I shared a good sense of humor, I replied, "Why don't you ring your tail around a flag pole." My mother intercepted the letter and never showed it to Dad. She scolded me for being disrespectful and told me to immediately write another letter. To this day I regret that Dad never saw the letter. He would have enjoyed it.

A few weeks before I was going to start the summer semester my advisor, Joe Hootman, called me and said if I took seventeen hours that summer I could be a senior in the fall and graduate the following June. He said I would only have twelve hours of class work and he would check my work on the other five hours. He meant that he would merely go over my outlines of my chapters in two economic courses and give me grades accordingly. Joe gave me a B in each course, but I think if I would have taken them conventionally I would have received an A. One of my other courses was a five-hour general science course taught by two professors. Three weeks were spent on chemistry, three weeks on biology, three weeks on physics, three weeks on astronomy, and three weeks on botany. The course met at three o'clock in the afternoon and nothing was more miserable than attending a course on a hot Saturday afternoon. The only good thing about this course was that Charlotte sat next to me throughout the course. I was almost positive I had flunked the course but the two professors must have graded on the curve. I received a B and thanked my lucky stars. The older I get the more I'm inclined to believe that often grades are issued depending on the whim of the professor.

During the end of the spring trimester and the end of the summer trimester there were two important events—one was V-E Day, the other was V-J Day. Since I will never forget these days I know my readers will enjoy hearing what the atmosphere was on the campus at that time.

The first of these days will go down in history as V-E Day. At Culver-Stockton, the Almighty played an important part in the first signs of peace. He gave us one of those rare May days, which is especially adapted for reflective thinking. As I remember it, I was laboring over a final exam, when the ringing of church bells distracted my trend of thought. Unconsciously, I arose, walked to the window and looked far beyond the locks into the flats of Illinois. At the open window, a gentle breeze silently whispered, "Peace is coming," and the warmth of the sun seemed to put living blood into the prophecy of the whispering wind.

The second, and probably the most important of the two days, will be recorded in the annals of history by future generations as V-J Day. The morning of this momentous day broke with a raging fury. The sun was hotter than the well known "Rising Sun" of Japan. Not a breath of air stirred all during the day and your moist skin served as very effective flypaper. Everyone was in a dither, waiting, hoping, praying for the inevitable message of the unconditional surrender of the Japanese Empire. Since this was a rare occasion, a radio was blaring away in the dining room of Culver Hall when all the summer school students entered for their evening meal. Just after grace was said, President Truman announced the long-awaited news. After the lump was cleared from everyone's throat, the thirty-some-odd students made more noise than a thousand of the groundskeeper's tractors.

The same evening the chorus put on their summer concert. Even though the air was oppressive, the heat was forgotten when the choir opened its program with the Star-Spangled Banner. Never before had that song meant so much to me as it did that night. After the recital I leisurely strolled down Lewis Street to town with the idea of quenching my thirst. To my disappointment every store in Canton was closed; but, for some reason I couldn't get mad, even if I was wringing wet after walking from the Hill. The next morning the Christian Church bulged with the citizens of Canton. President McDonald delivered the war eulogy, wisely pointing out that our enemies had been God's children, and consequently, there was no room for hatred, anger and contempt.

Although I expected no sympathy and never will, I think everyone should know how much extra energy a cerebral palsy person uses in his daily life. Merely walking uses about three times as much energy as the ordinary person. This is true for dressing, bathing, eating, speaking, walking, writing and typing. Cerebral palsy persons are constantly aware of every move we make and are forced to think where to put one's arm or leg, all of which functions come naturally to an ordinary person. A few of the tricks I learned were to use a button hook to fasten my buttons on my shirts, use hook-on ties, and wear loafers that did not require shoe strings. Even with these aides I spent twice as much time preparing myself to look presentable than the average person. One thing cerebral palsy persons are forced to tolerate are the stares of others, and comments made by young children and those who are ignorant. So much for that. Let's go on with something more interesting.

After a two week break I returned to the campus to begin my senior year. Thank the Lord, we went back to the semester basis and there were no more Saturday classes—what a relief. I spent most of the Saturdays taking my laundry box down to the post office, my cleaning to the cleaners, and other mundane things. My courses that year were all advanced studies including business law, corporation finance, applied psychology, etc.

Chuck and his roommate Don were next door and they frequently pounded on the wall just to annoy me. In the boys' washroom there was a tin enclosure with three spigots. Frequently, we would shower at the same time. Chuck would get at one spigot, and Don at the other far spigot. Having me in the middle they would turn their water on cold and turn it directly on me from both sides. The dirty dogs!

One other favorite sport of the boys was to fire up the furnace so high that the only thing that came out of the spigots was steam. When you entered in the room it was like a dense fog. During that period one of the other sports of the boys was to roll Coke bottles down the halls on the wood floors. Especially at night when the housemother was sleeping. One other memorable moment was one night when I was in a noisy bull session, directly above the housemother's room. When leaving our rooms we were always supposed to wear a robe over our pajamas. However, that night I was only in my pajamas when the housemother knocked on the door to quiet us down. I got behind the door. Unfortunately, my shadow showed on the floor. She asked, "Who's behind the door?" I replied, "It's me, Mother." Nothing more was ever said. One other incident was when Mother Yaeger baked the monthly birthday cake. Instead of locking it in the pantry as she should have, she left it in the open kitchen. It was half gone by the time we ate supper. She cried and told us we were not appreciative of her efforts. I really didn't have much sympathy for her, since she had raised a son of her own and knew how boys acted. I might add that Mother Yaeger's son was in the army. During the winter semester all the rooms in the dorm were filled; but for some reason I had the only private room. Since the fraternity houses were closed, each fraternity was given one room on the second floor to hold their meetings. At that time I was president of the inter-fraternity council and did what I could to hold hazing down to a minimum. But I did not escape hazing when I joined Lambda Chi. When I was initiated, I was taken out to a field in the rear of the campus and was rolled around a little bit. I am proud to say that the Lambda Chi national fraternity has now outlawed hazing and drinking. More and more of the national fraternities are following suit.

One of the students that entered Culver-Stockton in the fall of '45 was Bill Black, later known as Clay Mundey. Bill attended Culver only a year before he became a singer with Gene Krupa's band. As most bands do, Bill traveled with the band on buses from engagement to engagement and was introduced to drugs and alcohol. As most professional people, Clay had his ups and downs and ended up living in a tenement in the Italian district of New York. I was privileged to spend some time in Bill's tenement building and I really got an education, which I will relate further on in the book.

The Sunday before Thanksgiving we had our annual Thanksgiving dinner. The next day the cook made turkey stew. Unfortunately, she did not refrigerate the turkey. One or two hours after we ate, we were all fighting over the three stools in the boys' washroom. I need not mention that we all had a bad case of food poisoning, but I recovered enough to go home for Thanksgiving.

Late in December of 1945, the day before Christmas vacation, I returned to the boys' dorm after my classes. I looked out of my window and across the road and I saw a barnyard that reminded me of the manger of the Christ Child. After donning my shirt, tie and coat that we were required to wear for the evening meal as a matter of discipline, I went downstairs for my Christmas supper. In the evening many of the boys plodded through the snow to serenade the girls while the electric star on the administration building dome shown brightly.

The next afternoon after classes, I enthusiastically packed my grip and trudged down through the snow to the railroad station, which was about thirty feet from the Mississippi River. Before long I could hear the faint whistle of the Mark Twain Zephyr, which was one of the first diesel powered trains. Since all the St. Louis students went home at the same time, often some had to stand in the aisle. Fortunately, for me, Mom and Dad always treated me to a parlor car seat. This was quite a luxury because it had a snack bar and comfortable lounge chairs. When I boarded the train I looked back and saw the star on the dome shining brightly. The thought ran through my mind, "O little town of Bethlehem/How still we see thee lie."

As the Mark Twain Zephyr pulled into the St. Louis train yard at Union Station, it had to wait fifteen minutes to be assigned a track. It was a war year and every track was being used for trains bringing soldiers home for the Christmas furlough. As my train slowly backed into the assigned track I could see Mom and Dad waiting for me at the gate. The station was bustling with every kind of humanity, elbow to elbow, and I eagerly looked forward to seeing the old homestead. I was looking forward to my ten days of vacation as being happy and carefree; however, Mother went to pieces preparing the Christmas meal for our small family of eight. For the rest of my short vacation I was required to eat breakfast at 7:30 and always felt on edge. This was one more sign of Mother's oncoming mental illness.

When I returned to Canton I felt quite confident and knew that I would graduate in the spring. I prepared for the final exams and breezed through them without difficulty.

Early in February, my last semester, Coach Harrington, the basketball coach, approached me and said, "Slick, Friday night we are playing Westminster College at Fulton. I would love to have you ride over with the team and sit on the bench. I want to show those damn fools what a horrible mistake they made." Naturally it was a thrill for me to ride with the team and to see a few of my old friends at Westminster. To put icing on the cake, our team beat the hell out of Westminster. It was a cold night in February and I will never forget the thrill it gave me.

My last semester at Culver was a real joy and pleasurable. Although I continued to outline every chapter of every textbook, I learned to only put down the more important points and this gave me much more free time to socialize and to broaden my outlook on life. Professor Blalock and Professor Leftwich continued to impress on me that a person's character depends on one's conditioning and interaction with other people. Professor Blalock was also the minister of the local Christian Church and he preached his theories in every sermon he gave. I attended his sermons infrequently because I always knew what he was going to say. Professor Leftwich pounded home that the only way we would ever have world peace would be for us to have one world government, one world religion, one world language and one world race. In some respects, we are gradually turning towards some of his theories; but it will be centuries and centuries if we ever comply to everything he preached. Don't you think it would be rather dull and uninteresting if we were all the same? When a person is raised in one religion and one culture, he acquires a distinct characteristic that should be respected by all individuals. If this is done we could eliminate all religious wars—I'm referring to the ones in Ireland, Bosnia, Palestine and Israel.

After being rebuffed by a Christian Science school and by a Presbyterian college, my faith in formal religion waivers from time to time. I believe that true religion is how a person acts from hour to hour and from day to day. I know too many people that go to church Sunday after Sunday and then act atrociously throughout the week. I do my best to be considerate of everyone at all times and to be happy and cheerful.

One of the traditions at Culver-Stockton was the annual "flunk day" in the spring of the year. The seniors were allowed to pick the day and no one knew when it would come except for the cook who had to prepare the picnic lunch. On whatever day the seniors decided upon, the bells would ring early in the morning and all classes were dismissed for the day. All the students went to the back campus for lunch and the rest of the day they were free to do whatever they wanted. Charlotte and I enjoyed being together for the whole day and that evening we walked down to the river and stopped at the drug store for our usual sand storm.

A few weeks before graduation, Charlotte's parents, who lived in Palmyra, Missouri, invited Mom and Dad up for Sunday dinner. The Wildmans were wholesome, small-town people, just like their daughter. In a few days I received a letter from Mom saying that although the Wildmans were nice, they were small-town people and would not fit into their world. At that time, I had no means of supporting myself and had to take their advice. In retrospect, I should have put up a fight and should have put love before finances. Palmyra is a delightful small town, the county seat of Marion County. Mom and Dad could have given me the money left over from the trusts Aunt Tillie set up for my college education. I feel that I could have opened a small business in Palmyra, married Charlotte, raised a nice family and lived happily ever after. On the other hand, I probably would not have been able to display my leadership ability, which I did in later life. However, I really think happiness is more important.

Nick and I would frequently walk to town on Saturday afternoon. If we were accompanied by a third person I would get on the one side and Nick would get on the other. Then we would say, "I'm Nick, I'm Slick. Who is this prick between us."

One of the courses I took my last semester was political parties. It was taught by Dr. Messamore. There were three in the class including myself and two basketball players. The class was mainly a discussion group and the two basketball players could care less. Naturally I got an A out of the course and heaven knows what he gave the other two. If he passed them it was a true gift of sympathy.

In those archaic days all seniors were required to take a written and oral comprehensive examination before given permission to graduate. Most students studied furiously before the examination and literally sweated. I didn't do any reviewing and thought, after earning As and Bs, I would be well prepared for whatever might come. On the written examination I was given the choice of two out of five essay questions to answer. I knew I did well and looked forward to my oral examination with pleasure.

The morning of my oral examination, I walked down to the local drug store and bought three cigars. After lunch I dressed and slowly walked up the Hill. I will always remember that afternoon was warm and breezy. I entered the room to face the music. After I was asked a few asinine questions, it turned into a typical bull session. However, to keep things on the up and up I was asked to leave the room while they made their decision. I almost laughed in their faces but instead I said, "May I say something before I leave?" After gaining their permission, I said, "Professor Hootman, you taught me economics, here have a free cigar. Dr. Leftwich, you are a sociology professor, have a free cigar and sit around and chew the bull. And Professor Blalock, you taught me psychology, and I hope to God you think this is good psychology." Naturally, in a minute or two they came out of the room and told me I would graduate. For many years to come whenever I returned to campus they would want to know if I brought them any more free cigars.

On Sunday evening, June 3, 1946, the baccalaureate service was held at the local Christian Church. Reverend MacAllister, minister of the Webster Groves Christian Church, and a long-time friend of mine, delivered the address.

Monday morning, June 4, I proudly donned my cap and gown and walked up the Hill to join the processional into the gymnasium where the graduation ceremony was held. Gov. Phil Donnelly was the graduation speaker and after fifty years I don't remember a word he said. Therefore, I am going to take this opportunity to relate what I would say to today's graduates, after having lived for fifty years since my graduation.

Progress

Trustees, President Strong, faculty, graduates, parents, students and friends: For the next few minutes I am going to speak on what progress has been made in various fields since my graduation fifty years ago. First of all, may I call your attention to this modern campus. When I attended Culver-Stockton, there were the boys' dorm, the girls' dorm, the gymnasium, and the administration building. That was it. Now may I call your attention to the new gymnasium, the old gymnasium, which has been turned into a first-class business facility, the Campbell auditorium, the Robert W. Brown Building of Fine Arts, and the various residences for the students.

You graduating seniors have also made progress by meeting all the requirements for a college degree. Some of you are graduating with honors and many of you are not being recognized as outstanding students. However, I realize that many of you have expended more energy in your course of work than those graduating with honors. May I remind you that many of our famous leaders, scientists and inventors never saw the inside of a college. A college degree simply gives you a little edge in the field of your endeavors. However, it does not assure you of success or monetary rewards. It is up to you to apply your knowledge to your job.

At this point many of you will become supervisors, employers, managers, and entrepreneurs. To be successful in these positions, you must show respect for those who work under you. At all times you should be interested in their problems and try to alleviate their worries as much as possible. Also, you should use their capabilities to their fullest extent and never be hesitant to give them a deserved compliment.

Although Germany, Russia and Japan are no longer a threat to world peace, my generation has not completely eliminated conflicts from the world. After the end of World War II, the United Nations was born. At that time I thought it would be the solution to all future conflicts. Unfortunately, it has become very ineffective and a financial burden to the United States. However, I believe that if the United Nations could be made more powerful and respected by all nations, it would be much more effective as a peace keeper of the world.

Very little progress has been made in developing social relationships. Divorces are rampant. Families continue to be torn apart and people are still living in undesirable conditions. One of the greatest things you can contribute to society is to help alleviate and solve some of these social problems. You can start your crusade with your own family. Always treat your partner with loving understanding and raise your children to have a thirst for education. No matter how busy you might become, always find time to spend your recreation time with your children and participate in their activities, like Boy Scouts, Girl Scouts, etc.

As an educated person you are obligated to be a leader in your community: Take an active part in your church, become a leader of any service organization you might join, and use your influence in any local government affairs.

In closing, I want to say to the graduates, you might think you are fixed for life. However, you are just on the threshold of living; you will have a lot to experience and many problems to solve. Although my generation has made very little progress toward world peace, it is my fervent desire that you are more successful than we have been. Just think, if we were not required to spend money for implements of war, how much money we could save to help the poor and less fortunate of the world. Never become too satisfied with your accomplishments. Always strive to improve yourself and the environment in which you live. I know you will all make progress throughout your life and never become self-satisfied. God bless you and God speed in your quests for progress in all fields of living. Thank you.

Immediately after graduation, my parents, my two aunts, and my uncle had their pictures taken with me on the quadrangle. I was very proud of my accomplishments and, like I said after high school graduation, I had no regrets. I gave college everything I had and consequently had an inner satisfaction of a job well done. Since I had so much to take home, Mom and Dad loaded it in the car and with my two other relatives, there was no room for me. Therefore, I stayed a few days longer and brought a fraternity brother home with me on the train. I spent the last few days in Canton walking down to the river and in the evenings strolling along the tree-lined streets. I knew from that moment I would always have a warm spot in my heart for the little town of Canton.

In retrospect, I wonder why none of the faculty encouraged me to attend graduate school or advised me as to what type of occupation I would be best suited. There was enough money left over in my aunt's trust to accomplish the task without being a financial burden to the family. I probably could have earned a law degree and made considerably more as a lawyer in a large law firm doing research. On the other hand, I would have been somewhat of a hermit and would not have acquired the various leadership roles I have experienced.

As my fraternity brother, Robert Kistler, and I boarded the train for St. Louis, the thought entered my mind that I had been the first cerebral palsy person that Culver-Stockton had mainstreamed and graduated. I'm not sure but I think to this day no other cerebral palsy person has graduated from the old Culver.

After returning home, Mom let Bob drive her car and we hit all the tourist attractions of St. Louis. Like so many of my college associates, Bob and I have remained friends throughout our lifetimes. The week passed very quickly and on the following weekend Mom and Dad decided it was time for me to go to work.

In 1963, Culver-Stockton decided to honor five alumni every year; one in the field of science, one in religion, one in history, one in sociology, and one in economics. Therefore, since I was recognized in 1965 I was one of the first of fifteen ever to be so honored at the age of forty-two. I think one reason for them to elect me was that they weren't sure how long I would survive.

On the morning of the recognition day in April we formed a processional to march into the gymnasium. Because of my inability to keep up with the processional they slowed it down to a crawl. However, we finally made it to the stage and when President Fred Helsabeck presented me with the alumni medallion, he whispered, "This is not only for your accomplishments in business but for the wonderful understanding you have given your mother in her mental illness."

In the afternoon I was to meet with the seniors in economics. However, because they thought I would have difficulty speaking, they had me write a paper to be read to the students in Economics. However, it was so well received that they asked the entire student body to come to the chapel and my economics professor read the paper to the audience. I divided my paper into three parts. The first part was dedicated to education where I emphasized that education is the ability to know where to go for what you want to know. I also gave them simplified definitions for psychology, logic, philosophy, religion, political science and sociology.

In the second part of my paper I urged the students to travel to see the wonders of our country and to appreciate and see the beauty of nature. I pointed out one country store I visited in rural Vermont. It was a true general store and it was a throwback to our past history.

The third part of my paper was devoted to my income tax business. I emphasized that I always tried to explain everything to my clients so they would have a better understanding of the law. I always tried to come down to their level and I always showed sympathy in their frustrations. Throughout the years I gained more and more clients because of my warm approach to their problems.

In the evening a supper was held for the five alumni who received the awards. We each were asked to make a short speech on the subject of our award. I went back to my old speech and asked, "Would I be here tonight if I had not had a wonderful mother and father who taught me to stand on my own two feet? Would I be here tonight if I had not had the opportunity to receive a wonderful education? Would I be here tonight if I had not been born in America where everyone has an equal opportunity? And forthly, would I be here tonight without the help of God?" The speech was well received and I received a standing ovation.

Several weeks later I entertained the St. Louis Alumni at Westborough Country Club. After we met, President Helsabeck came up and asked me, "Have you ever thought of leaving money to the college?" At this point I informed him of the three trusts that had been set up for the college in 1948; however, I told him I did not want it to be known until after I received the award.

In 1991, the college came to me and told me that they wanted to establish *The Warren E. Gerlach Chair of Accounting,* if I could match a challenge of a $50,000 matching gift. I flatly refused because I told them I did not want my friends to feel obligated. However, several weeks later my secretary, Joanne Auinbauh, said, "Why don't you let them try. If your friends don't want to give, they won't give." The glorious outcome was that over 120 of my friends contributed over $50,000 and the college received the matching $50,000 from the Herrick Foundation. But to my amazement the vast majority of the contributors were my high school and college classmates, who I hadn't seen for fifty years. One of the main contributors was Ed Knetzger, president of my junior high school class, who contributed a sizable amount and his company contributed the same amount. Another contributor was King "Barney" Barnett, who at age ninety-two wrote, "I was fortunate to have Warren in my biology class back in 1940. I was a better man for having him as a student." Several of the other donors were people I met on my travels. These people did not see me more than three or four times but I guess I made a lasting impression because even to this day they write and send me Christmas cards.

4
My Years in Business

Monday morning, I rode to work with Dad and was immediately given a desk with a calculator, price lists and told to check the calculations on the previous day's orders. Since most of the employees had watched me grow up, and since I was the only one in the office with a college degree, not a single person came over to welcome me to the company. Even the president, who was a teenager when I was born and had watched my progress, failed to greet me warmly.

Acme Paper Company was on Eighth and Walnut in the heart of the warehouse district. There was a coffee company one block away and the aroma was always delightful. Acme Paper Company rented two whole floors of the building, which were used for the storage of paper that was eventually sold to printers. The office space was long and narrow, directly visible when you entered the door. It was comprised of three sets of four desks facing each other. The only ventilation we had was old-fashioned fans. The floors were worn wood. Behind the office was the cutting room, which had two large paper cutters, capable of cutting a thousand sheets of paper with one fast drop of the blade. Even the warehousemen had watched me grow up and I think everyone in the place rather resented my invasion of their firm. True to my work ethic, I pounded that damn calculator for eight hours with an hour's break for lunch. Dad sat directly behind me and smoked his pipe and okayed every order for credit rating. He had a bookkeeper to do the actual bookkeeping and for the last couple of years he acted as a public relations officer for the company. He was very active in the downtown Kiwanis Club. One day Dr. Franc McCleur, the president of Westminster College, spoke at Dad's Kiwanis Club. After his speech he was man enough to come up and say to Dad, "Mr. Gerlach, may I apologize to you, we made an awful mistake on Warren." At this point, I want to say that he also lost about $180,000 for the college since my aunt set up trusts for Culver-Stockton College that now have a value of approximately $450,000.

I continued to work on my calculator for three months. At this point my chest began to hurt and eventually I had to take a leave of absence. I thought it was my heart and I was examined by various doctors and found to be in excellent health. The problem was that the nerves in my chest had become so tight that they caused severe pain. These days even ordinary people who work constantly on computers will acquire repetitive-motion pain. Of course, on a cerebral palsy person the agony is about threefold. The pain continued for another three months and was not completely alleviated until my appendectomy operation.

Shortly thereafter one of the eastern paper mills wanted to have their own outlet in the worst way and they made an offer to the shareholders to purchase the stock for $240 a share. During the depression, Dad had purchased many shares from other stockholders for thirty dollars a share. It was quite a nice profit. When Dad received the money for the sale he luckily invested the money in mutual funds, which have grown throughout the years. At the time of the sale, the new owners assured Dad that he could stay on with the company, however, like many companies are prone to do, in a few months they sent Dad a letter that his services were no longer needed. They agreed to pay Dad a monthly salary for a year. In 1948, after being secretary/treasurer of the company for thirty-eight years, Dad retired and was presented a gold watch from his fellow workers.

At the time of my appendicitis attack, Mom was in St. Anthony's Hospital for a hemorrhoid operation. Therefore when I became sick, Dad dropped me off at Aunt Blanche and Uncle Harry's on his way to work. Aunt Blanche called the doctor and the nurse said he would visit me in the afternoon. However, the nurse got the address wrong and when he didn't come by eight o'clock in the evening Aunt Blanche called his home since I was in pure agony.

"Thank God you called, I've been looking for your house all afternoon," he said. Dr. Kuenkel rushed over to the house, examined me quickly, put me over his shoulder, drove me to the hospital, and had me on the operating table within the hour. If a few more minutes had elapsed, the appendix would have burst. During my convalescence, Mrs. Dewey, the nurse that had attended Mother at my birth, came over and spent long hours with me until I was on the road to recovery. In those days, I was so spastic and perspired so much my back broke out in a horrible rash. As soon as I got up and walked around the rash disappeared.

While recovering from my operation and regaining my strength, I spent my idle time writing the following essays:

Gabriel & George

You know, George, with all the labor riots and other wars of greed and misunderstanding being waged down on earth, our working days are growing longer and longer. However, I believe that our newly arrived guests are perfectly contented, so let's see what is causing all the ruckus down below.

Nothing would make me happier, Gabriel.

Look over there, George, what do you see?

Why there is a manger, and over there are the three wise men gazing upon the star, and all the people are rejoicing. Lo and behold, that is the little town of Bethlehem.

No, George, you are wrong as to location and time. Remember, up here we never turn back the pages of time. If we did, we certainly couldn't maintain our eternal happiness. We aren't interested in man's past mistakes; but we do get a joy in seeing how each generation corrects previous misconceptions in the slow and painful process of evolution.

Okay, Gabriel, that's enough philosophy out of you for a week. Will you please tell me what I'm seeing.

George, I'm ashamed of you. Has it been too long ago for you to remember your college days? That manger is the same one you used to look at out of your window in the boys' dorm. At that time you just thought it was a dirty, unkempt barnyard; but, its hidden beauty was always there.

Stop it, Gabriel, you're making me hate my youth.

Your three wise men, George, are just three boys walking up from town after a late evening snack. And the star, don't you remember the star, which shined from the dome every Yuletide season.

Yes, I certainly do; but it certainly impresses me more now than it did when I was a student. Look at those three boys, arm in arm, just gazing at the star. Bet they belong to the same fraternity.

Wrong again, George. The one on the right is Don Whipper, president of the SIGs; in the middle is Bill Topper, rush chairman of the Delts, and on the left is Dave Doud, a Phi pledge.

Listen here, Gabriel, you can't make me believe that. Why, when I was down there, the SIGs, Delts and Phis had their own assigned street. If anyone trespassed, we mobbed him.

I know, George. I was right here looking down on you. Now, you can understand why I'm happy tonight. Only fifty years ago those three boys would have been walking separate streets, thinking of what evil trick they could pull on each other. Tonight, they are walking arm in arm, appreciating together the symbol of a glorious occasion. Yes, maybe they are three wise men.

Well, I'll be, if it isn't Pat Kinney getting out of the big sedan, which just stopped at the foot of the Hill. Old Pat was one of my classmates; must be in his seventies. He's grinning at that burning street light. Took the college authorities thirty years to think of that wire cage. Spoiled a lot of fun too. Weren't we devils in those days, Gabriel.

No truer words were ever spoken, George.

Holy cats! Pat is climbing those back-breaking steps. Why is he exerting all that effort when he could ride to the top of the Hill?

I imagine it's like this, George. Pat, as you know, was always a hustler. Long ago he discovered that you only get out of life what you put into it. Therefore, Pat is walking those steps tonight because he knows that by expending a little energy, he'll cherish this scene more deeply.

Gabriel, what Pat! He's almost to the top, four inches of snow are beneath his feet, his nose is nearly frozen; but he's still smiling.

Yes, Pat is rejoicing; for he is at peace with the world. The snow is sparkling in the moonlight, the star is imbuing him with that glorious vision of old, and the carols ringing from the chapel emphasize the midnight clear.

Now that Pat has strolled up the long winding walk, and is shivering in the wind-swept quadrangle, please tell me what Pat is thinking about, as he peers into the distant valley?

Frankly, George, your request is outside my powers. But, as I see Pat standing there in a silence of adoration, I imagine these words are running through his mind:

O little town of Bethlehem, how still we see thee lie;

Above thy deep and dreamless sleep, the silent stars go by;

Yet in thy dark streets shineth the everlasting light;

The hope and fears of all the years are met in thee tonight.

Character

Character is not a tangible thing, it sometimes cannot even be seen. It is something inside of you, which causes you to do certain things. Although it regulates your actions, this inside power can be changed by self-determination, by perseverance, and by a change of motives. I think that these three items are the basic principles of the term, character. Self-determination is probably the most challenging of the three. When a man makes up his mind to accomplish a goal and then accomplishes it without any dishonesty, he is certainly a man to be admired. I challenge every one of you to set a high goal for yourself and within the next few years see to it that you carry your own ball over the goal line. I assure you that all the effort you put into the task will not be in vain, because even the Good Book says, "Whatsoever a man soweth, so shall he reap."

Preserving, the second element of character, ties up in many ways with self-determination. We all know that the straight path is very narrow and often deceiving to the human eye. When you attempt to transverse it, you will find that the slightest misstep will throw you to the depths of wrongdoings. At this stage of the game do not give up, but on the other hand say to yourself, "I'll show the world that I am not licked and then go out and make a name for myself." While doing this, remember: Nothing pertaining to character is obtained from a silver platter. This character-building is a tedious matter of perseverance, why not adopt this motto: "If you do not succeed at first, try, try again."

By this time in your life I hope you have realized the fact that no one is made perfect or does anyone have perfect motives by which he is guided. When you discover that you have a bad motive, immediately attempt to change it. From practical experience I have noticed a lot of bitter resentment around school. Resentment is the cause for most of our wars, because one country resents the superiority of the other. I am sorry to say this, but I do believe that this same condition exists within the walls of this mighty institution. If this is allowed to continue in our school, we will probably have all of our privileges taken away from us. Nobody wants this to happen so why not change our motives. Smile at the people in the hall, keep your chin high and your head low, and last but not least, be considerate to the other fellow, because he is the fellow who can cause you the most agitation.

In closing I would like to say that the simplest way to develop character is to "Do unto the other person as you would have them do unto you."

In February of 1947, I went back and worked as receiving clerk for the Board of Education. On that job I could use my large coordination, which was a lot easier than using my small muscles on a calculator. Of course I had to get some boys out of study hall to carry the various equipment and supplies to the various rooms. However, I worked hard and kept good track of all the supplies. I was receiving forty cents an hour and asked the business manager for a raise. A week later, I was told that after August 31, my services were no longer needed. Being happy on the job and not really needy of the salary, my father went to see Mr. Steger, the high-strung and fiery superintendent of schools, and asked him to keep me on without a salary. Mr. Steger rather impolitely told Dad that he was running the show and thanked my dad to keep his nose out of his business. Mr. Steger's argument was that I had far too much education for such a menial job. In retrospect, he did me a big favor.

After I was home for a week or two Mom decided to mainstream me in a big way, and I mean big way. She put me in the car and drove me down to St. Louis Hills where there were eight-lane streets with practically no traffic. She put me behind the wheel, showed me the gas pedal and the four gears on the car. Then she said to go to it. After one wild turn I learned to control the speed of the car and that was the start of many, many happy years of driving. For years, no matter how nervous I was or under what strain, all I had to do was to get behind the wheel of my car and I was completely relaxed. Fortunately, in those days, a driver's license was not required, so I drove in traffic without passing any examination. My only little incident was the first time I tried to put Mom's car in our underground garage with my dad's car already there. Our driveway into the garage had a stone wall on each side with just inches to spare. The space in the garage was even less. It was tight. My first effort resulted in making a small dent in my father's car. Nothing was said and I navigated the driveway without incident from then on. In order to get the car out of garage into the street you had to make several "Y" maneuvers before you could get out into the street. It was good practice for driving in traffic.

My friend, Nick, who was the first person to approve of me for the fraternity, graduated from Culver in June of '47 and moved to St. Louis to take a job with the White Motor Company. Nick rented one room in the home of an elderly lady on Kingshighway and Arsenal. After work, Nick and I frequently went out for a ride in the evening. It was good practice for me and I learned how to shift gears without having the car leap forward. One real hot Sunday Mom invited Nick out for a Sunday dinner. Mom insisted on strict formality and when poor Nick came out in a brand new white T-shirt she ripped him apart for not wearing a dress shirt. I was so embarrassed that I'll never get the incident out of my mind.

In the fall of 1949, Nick moved over to 5095 Waterman Avenue to room with one of the former Culver-Stockton graduates who was attending mortuary school. His name was John Best Lewis, whose father owned the Lewis Brothers Funeral Home in Palmyra, Missouri. Once in a while they would invite me over for Saturday night supper and served a mulligan stew which was comprised of all of the leftovers in the icebox. One Saturday night Jack was returning from a fraternity initiation. He was running down the street when a police officer pulled up beside him. There had been a burglary in the neighborhood. The police officer asked him to get into the car and they took him over to the place where the burglary had occurred. The old woman said he was the guy and they threw Jack in jail and Jack said there was one steel bench to lay on and a toilet without a seat. The men on either side of his cell said they were not guilty either and in an hour or two the guards said, "Would you care to make a phone call?" Jack said he sure would and he called the dean of the college and told him his predicament. The dean of the college said, "I will be right down to bail you out." In the meantime the police got the old lady and brought her to the station and she said that Jack was not the guy. The next Monday, the dean told the whole class about the incident and everyone was amused.

One of the summers while Jack attended Culver-Stockton College he worked on the Mississippi River as a deckhand on the towboat *Minnesota*. The next summer he worked as a laborer on the *Dipper Dredge St. Paul* and also was sandblast foreman on the Canton Dam. One night while Jack was on duty, the captain in the pilot house asked Jack to bring him a cup of coffee. Jack, not knowing how to make coffee, put coffee grounds in a cup of hot water, stirred it up and took it up to the captain. The captain said, "Are you new?" Jack said, "I sure am." The captain took a swallow and threw the mess overboard and ordered Jack to wake up the cook at 3:00 A.M. and tell the cook to bring him a cup of coffee. Although the cook became irritated he became a friend of Jack's before the summer was over.

When Jack graduated from mortician school he worked in Kansas City and would return every weekend to St. Louis. On Friday evening he would date one girl and tell her he had to be back the next day. Then on Saturday he would take another girl out. The scheme worked until the girls compared notes and found they were both dating the same guy at the same time. The only good thing about the whole episode was that one of the girls, Barb Stout, introduced Nick to Ginna Roth, a student nurse at St. Luke's Hospital, who in later years became his wife. When Barb introduced Nick to Ginna she told Ginna that Nick was rather fast. Nick and Ginna got along quite well and went steady until they got married in November of 1952.

For years Jack's father and uncle ran the funeral home in Palmyra, Missouri. When the two older Lewis's retired, Jack and his cousin, George, took over the business. They had built a modern funeral home in Palmyra and both have retired recently. Now their sons run the business and are very successful.

Nick knew Wally Haller and his mother adopted Nick as another son because she was a widow and Wally was in service. Mrs. Haller had an apartment and frequently had Nick, Ginna and I over for supper and evening fun. Mrs. Haller was a legal secretary and was very sharp. My mother resented me going over to her house and criticized Mrs. Haller every time possible. Mrs. Haller's name was Glennie Ethel and we often referred to her as General Electric, since her initials were G. E. I spent many happy evenings in her apartment and she kept track of me for many years.

Ginna's nursing class put on a carnival in the basement of the nurses' residence. I'll never forget when Nick and I attended the carnival, one of the southern girls was in charge of the house of horror. When she yelled out, "Come to the Horror House" it sounded like "whore house" and it stuck in my memory for many years to come. Another funny incident was when Nick and Ginna went out on a Saturday night before Easter. Ginna never drank and that one night she had one or two and got deathly sick. She couldn't return home to her strict Lutheran parents until she sobered up. Therefore Nick and Ginna rode around all night until she puked in Forest

Park instead of attending Easter services with her family. To this day I always phone Ginna before Easter and remind her of the one Easter she hopes I'll forget about, but I never will.

While in St. Louis for two years, Nick would go back to his parents' farm which was a few miles outside of Lewistown, Missouri. Lewistown is a small country town with old wooden buildings and farmers sitting outside of the various buildings. I was invited up to spend a couple of days and I'll never forget my first trip. Mom Nichols was a roly-poly jolly woman who took me under her wing and treated me royally. She had another son, Sammy, who has a hearing and speech disability and attended the School for the Hearing Impaired at Fulton, Missouri.

On my first trip to the farm I followed Nick's directions over the old country road, which was full of ruts. On the way I passed the old, wooden, one-room schoolhouse which was no longer used because many rural areas had consolidated into school districts, which provide a much better education for everyone.

My first visit to the farm was before they had running water inside or outside the house. On the first day there it was extremely hot and I had to chew gum like mad when I used the old smelly outhouse. Of course, it was all new to me and I sure learned how the other half lived. In later years, they acquired running water and modern facilities. Dad Nichols was a hard worker and in planting and harvesting seasons he would work from sunrise to sundown. However, I guess the hard work never hurt him because he is now living in a nursing home at the age of ninety-three. After a few years Mom and Dad Nichols built a home next to theirs for her mother. After she passed away I slept in the home when I visited them. Dad Nichols was a big tease and I'll never forget one winter night he put an alarm clock under my bed and set it for three o'clock in the morning. Naturally when it went off, it scared the devil out of me and when I came over to the main house for breakfast I was determined not to crack a smile. However, I couldn't help it and we all got a big kick out of it. Many years later I made a special trip to Lewistown to help them celebrate their fiftieth wedding anniversary.

Nick was transferred by White Motor Company to Oklahoma City. He rented an apartment at 836 East Street. The apartment was Spanish style with three rooms and a small patio. While Nick was still a bachelor, I drove down to spend a weekend with him. At this time the turnpike had not been built and old Highway 66 was badly in need of repair. Later on it was a real joy to drive over the Turner Turnpike, which saved several hours. I spent the weekend with Nick. The highlight was attending an Oklahoma University football game. During the era, Oklahoma was ranked number one and everyone in Oklahoma was football crazy. When we attended the game, Nick had tickets purchased by the White Motor Company. Our seats were on the very top of the Snakepit, which was the name given to the Oklahoma Bowl. About half way through the game a breeze started to blow in from the north and I nearly froze to death. That same breeze often blows red dust from the prairies into all the apartments and homes in Oklahoma City.

The first night in the apartment I shared the only bed with Nick. In about an hour the bed came apart and we had to get up and make repairs. I told Nick, "Don't ever tell Ginna I broke her bed."

After being in Oklahoma City for one or two years Nick and Ginna were finally married. They wanted to include me in their wedding party but I thought it was advisable to remain in the audience. I visited them twice a year and each time I would board the train in Webster Groves on a Friday evening, sleep in a roomette on the train and arrive in Oklahoma City early Saturday morning. Nick and Ginna would be waiting for me and we would cram in two days of fun up to the time I boarded the train on Sunday evening to return to Webster Groves. The train arrived in Webster Groves at 8 A.M. Monday morning and Dad would pick me up and drive me directly to work at Kaegel Drug.

When Nick got married, he was as skinny as a telephone pole. Shortly thereafter, he was diagnosed as having a severe case of diabetes. Fortunately, Ginna was a nurse and even to this day keeps Nick's diabetes under control. For over a year Nick's legs were so painful he could hardly walk and had to quit working for a while. After he started to improve he went to work for the Harper Oil Company and became one of the executives for over thirty years. It was another case of where a student who just made average grades became quite successful.

Nick and Ginna moved from their apartment into a comfortable home. The neighborhood began to deteriorate so they sold their house and moved into a Spanish style home with three bedrooms, two baths, and a lovely yard. For many years I spent my Thanksgiving holidays with them. On the Friday after Thanksgiving, Oklahoma University always played Nebraska University. In Oklahoma City they practically had a national holiday. Most businesses closed and everybody watched the games on TV. Naturally, just to spite Ginna, I always rooted for the other team. On Saturdays and Sundays, I always took the family out for meals and those weekends are etched in my mind. They always regretted that I could not come down after I broke my hip, because for years I would help them rake up their leaves, which covered their front yard. In the front yard they had a persimmon tree that made horrible spots in the driveway. In self-defense I always parked my car on the street. I didn't want that stuff on my car.

At first I drove down over the old 66, a two-lane highway. In later years the Will Rogers and Turner Turnpikes were built, which saved many hours of travel. One time on the Turner Turnpike I stopped at a rest stop for lunch. I came back out and started on my merry way. About eight miles down the highway I saw a highway patrolman flashing his red lights. Naturally I pulled over on the side of the road and he asked to see my driver's license. After he inspected the license, I told him I had cerebral palsy. He replied, "Oh, I understand now, we had a report that you were drunk."

Instead of getting mad, I replied, "Thank you for doing your job, I appreciate your caring about my well being." The officer gave me a pat on the back and wished me well.

For many years Nick and Ginna attempted to have a child. Ralph was finally born and I enjoyed watching his development throughout the years. I thought he was going to be a spoiled brat but I was happily mistaken. He attended the University of Missouri-Rolla and received his master's degree from Oklahoma University. Ralph married Melanie and lives in South Carolina where he is employed as an environmental engineer for DuPont. Ralph has written many articles, and his services have been requested throughout the country. I am very proud of his accomplishments, and am always thrilled when he pays me a visit.

When I drove home from Oklahoma City I always spent an evening in Bixby, Oklahoma, with my grade school chum, Edwin Earsom. In spite of his infantile paralysis and the burden of wearing braces and a cast around his body, Ed taught music and conducted a marching band for eighteen years at all the high school football games. One year the band was declared the state championship band. He accomplished this feat by conducting the band in their maneuvers from a high chair. In later years Ed taught biology and physiology in the high school. Every time I would arrive in Bixby about one o'clock, Ed would invite me to address his class. I always gave a motivational speech and made all of the students aware of the beautiful environment in which they were living.

Ed certainly has mainstreamed himself into ordinary living and I marvel at his ability to overcome his physical handicaps.

Several weeks after Mr. Steger fired me, I happened to be lingering around the new drug store that had been opened. Mr. Kaegel, the owner, had worked for the Ambrose-Mueller Drug Store on the corner of Elm and Big Bend for several years. He had the guts to open his own store about a half-block away. While I was lingering I practiced my old habit of straightening up the magazines. Mr. Kaegel approached me and said, "How would you like to do this on a daily basis. I need somebody to check in magazines and to keep the rack straight." I was happy to do a menial job and this was the start of a five-year stint with Kaegel Drug. The store was almost a cracker box, it was so small, and space was tight.

In a few weeks I started to file the charges, then I started to get out the monthly statements, then in addition I started counting the money and going to the bank every day. I worked myself into a full-time job and gained the respect of Mr. Kaegel, whom I will now refer to as Uncle Al. Uncle Al paid no attention to my handicap. When we were short of help he let me sell cigars, cigarettes and other items at the front register. I always greeted everyone in a friendly manner and gave them my usual grin. By such exposure I made many friends who came to me for their income tax work in later years. I had keys to the store and often worked at night and on Sundays in order to keep my work up to snuff. Of course, it also furnished me with an excuse to get out of the house, since conditions in my home continued to deteriorate.

We had some very interesting employees working at that time. The first pharmacist was Mr. Halteman, a middle-aged man who used to love to talk about his home town, Pocatella, Idaho. We had a little difficulty keeping him sober. He used to hide his beer bottle behind a big gallon container of medicine. He was always able to do the job, but you were able to tell when he was imbibing. One of the relief pharmacists was Taylor Lindhorst, who in later years became the dean of the School of Pharmacy in St. Louis. The other relief pharmacist was Frank Martin, who later married the fountain girl, Pat. They moved to Mississippi. The other interesting character was Bessie Lindhorst, Taylor's aunt, who made all the deliveries. She was very independent and sometimes made the deliveries to suit herself rather than be prompt. When Mr. Kaegel was out of the store, I tried to prod her on but it was just like talking to a stone wall.

Mr. Kaegel's wife was the former Jeanette Lipp, who had run a very successful dance studio. She was temperamental as hell and some mornings she would talk to me and other mornings completely ignore me with her nose stuck up in the air. Jeanette must have given Uncle Al fits because some mornings Uncle Al would open the backdoor of the store and for no reason at all rip everybody apart from head to toe. However, he never said boo to me because he knew damn well I could live without the job and he couldn't find anyone else to do what I was doing for the salary I was getting. In all fairness, I want to say Uncle Al could be a gentle person at other times. He could have gotten a lot more out of his employees if he had studied and practiced psychology and sociology.

The office space was in one back corner of the store. It was the size of an office desk. Since the business was growing I needed more room to operate. Consequently, Uncle Al rented an old house across the street. I used the front room for an office and the other three rooms were used to store bulk items. We had an intercom between the office and the store so if anyone wanted to know what they owed I could tell them. In those days Dad was retired and he was helping me at the end of the month getting out statements. Although I had a business degree, I always had a desire to learn more—and I still do. Therefore, I took a course in investments at Washington University in the evening. The instructor was a stock broker and he predicted that although the Dow Jones was at 500 it would go to 1400 some day. We all thought he was nuts.

Mr. Kaegel's business prospered and he bought ground across the street. Shortly thereafter he began construction of a drug store eight times larger than the old store. At the new store we had a private office with Uncle Al's desk on one end and mine on the other. Every day at noon the fountain girl brought in Uncle Al's lunch and he topped it off with a "boilermaker" (bourbon & beer). After the conditions I had been working in, the new office seemed like heaven. I was relieved of the job of checking in magazines and Mr. Halteman's wife, Eleanor, was hired to help me with the book work.

At this point the number of daily prescriptions grew and grew. Consequently, another young pharmacist, Ray Klotz, was employed and became a dedicated and reliable employee. Ray had just returned from the army and walked two miles to put in an application for a job at Kaegel's as a pharmacist. He was an excellent worker and I trust he was the best employee Al Kaegel ever had, besides me. We gradually became acquainted with each other and decided to take vacations together. Our first vacation was out West. One Sunday morning we were at the Grand Canyon and Ray had his choice of either going to mass or riding a donkey down into the canyon. He probably would never have this opportunity again, however, because of his devotion to his religion, Ray attended mass and, in my opinion, missed the golden opportunity of seeing all the beautiful formations that God had created. That August when we were traveling there were many fasting days when Ray was not allowed to eat meat. On our way home, we stopped to stay with Nick and Ginna overnight. When we entered the house it was the first time Ray ever met my good friends, Nick and Ginna. The first words out of Ray's mouth were, "I can't eat meat today." Ray is the most wonderful person anyone would want to meet and he certainly did not realize how this sounded. I thought to myself, why make an issue of it. If you can't eat meat when it is served to you just leave it lie. In later years when the Pope allowed Catholics to eat meat every day except Good Friday and Ash Wednesday, I often think to myself, what is the difference between now and then.

One summer Ray and I took a trip to Florida. We went by way of New Orleans where we spent one whole day. In the morning we took the Greyline tour, which is the best way to see any big city. On the tour all the important spots were pointed out including the graves which are above ground because the city is below sea level. We saw all the familiar tourist spots including Canal Street and the French Quarter. In the evening we took the nightclub tour which was comprised of four different clubs. At each club there was a girlie show, and we were required to buy a drink. In those days I continued to be on the wagon and it burned my soul to spend a dollar at each place for a lousy Coke. The tour ended at the French Market about 2:00 in the morning, where we were served delicious French rolls and hot coffee. From New Orleans we drove along the coast to Biloxi where Jim Cutter was stationed. At the time Jim was an MD in the army and we were treated to a dinner in the Officers Club. At the time Jim only had one child and every few years when I visited him throughout the country, he had one more, one more, one more, etc., when he finally gave up at number seven. Biloxi is known as the sewer of America and I heartily agree. From there we drove to Miami and then on up to Fort Lauderdale where we spent the night. Our next night we spent in St. Augustine where we took the usual horse and buggy ride. St. Augustine turned out to be a complete disaster. In the morning, Ray, being a rabid Catholic, insisted on attending the 10 A.M. mass. I said, "Put your things in the car, I will put mine in and I'll pick you up at the church after mass." Mass was over at 11 A.M. and Ray hopped in the car and we headed up the road.

We had gone exactly 200 miles when Ray turned around and said, "Oh my God, I left my suit carrier in the motel. We must go back and pick it up."

"Hell no," I said, "we'll wait here and have it sent up by bus."

Ray replied, "I have all my clothes in the bag and we are going back." Since Ray was driving, what could I do! We drove back to St. Augustine and picked up his damn suitcase. We drove back to the same spot where we had been approximately six hours prior.

In later years, Ray fell in love with a lovely girl who had a severe case of diabetes. Before Mary and Ray married, Dr. and Mrs. Martin, Mary's parents, had Ray and I to their home frequently for Sunday barbecue. Dr. Martin was a happy and understanding man and worked as a dentist for the Veterans Administration in the Old Mart Building. I spent many Sundays at their hospitable home. After going with Mary Martin for several years, they got married. At that time Ray knew that Mary was going blind but he continued his devotion and took care of her until Mary's dying day. I went to her funeral which was on one of the bitterest cold days of the year. For some reason the heating in the church was not functioning correctly and I really got a cold reception to a Catholic funeral.

Dr. and Mrs. Martin bought a condo after Mary died and had me out once a month for cocktails and supper. They were very understanding about my physical condition and treated me royally. In about a year Mrs. Martin developed heart trouble and the only way to try to save her life was by performing an operation. After struggling for four or five weeks after the operation, Mrs. Martin passed away. Dr. and Mrs. Martin were so attached to each other that upon her death, Dr. Martin started to drink heavily. One morning, Dr. Martin called Ray and said, "Ray come over quick, I'm in trouble. I'm dying." Ray rushed him to the hospital and they performed an operation on an aneurysm in his stomach, however, it was too late and Dr. Martin joined his wife in heaven. After their deaths Ray took his mother into his house and cared for her for many years until she died of leukemia. Ray is one of the most devoted persons I know. Now that I am in the nursing home, Ray comes to visit me and cheers me up every Sunday afternoon. If anyone is going to heaven, it is going to be Ray. I love his devotion to me and often marvel at the many sacrifices he has made during his life. The world needs more people like Ray. God bless him.

One summer Ray and I headed for Yellowstone National Park and stayed at the park's new motel lodge which was connected to a modern shopping area. Of course, one of the thrills of Yellowstone is seeing Old Faithful spouting her fountain on an hourly basis. From there, we went down to Jackson Hole where I had the privilege of viewing the Grand Teton mountains. They are always snow covered and a most picturesque site. One day we toured Virginia City and saw the old frontier buildings, which have remained untouched by human hands. On another trip, Ray and I headed north and saw the four stone faces carved on Mt. Rushmore. One must marvel at the patience it took the sculptor to make them so realistic. From there we went to the Badlands of South Dakota. I'll never forget one night we stayed in a primitive motel in Deadwood. The shower consisted of a round circle that did not produce much water. However, we survived and it was another occasion where you learn how the other half lives. Since that time, the town has acquired a few casinos and has prospered.

I admire Ray and still marvel at his devotion to his religion. Ray still takes a course led by a priest who stimulates the minds of the class members. No one should ever get too old to receive more education, and more ideas.

While working at Kaegel Drug, I took a night course at Washington University in retailing. The course paid big dividends. One Sunday afternoon while I was counting the cash, the main register was over ten dollars. I immediately looked in the change bag which each employee prepares for the next day. The bag was short ten dollars and I became very suspicious. I immediately called Uncle Al and told him what I thought was going on. We set the trap and the next day when everything checked out perfectly we knew that the pharmacist we suspected was shortening the register to the tune of $10 every day. The following day when the pharmacist reported for work Mr. Kaegel called him in to the office and asked for his key. He asked no questions and promptly left the store. I have no idea how long he had been doing this or how much money I saved Uncle Al by being alert. This pharmacist was of slight build and always had a cigarette hanging from the corner of his mouth. I never did care for him and it gave me extra pleasure to nail him.

The store prospered until the appearance of malls, where parking facilities were adequate. All Uncle Al had was street parking and in due time his son, Albert, who came into the business, had to close the store and operate a small pharmacy next door. It was a shame Uncle Al could not have seen the necessity of having adequate parking.

While working at Kaegel's I was notified by the Cerebral Palsy Association that they were having a swim party every Tuesday at the Missouri School for the Blind. It was a hot summer and I said, "Why not." After going two times I met Phoebe Anderson, the daughter of Edgar Anderson, curator of Shaw's Garden. I asked for a date and she immediately accepted with enthusiasm. The family lived in the residence in Shaw's Garden and I picked her up every night. We would either go to a drive-in show or smooch in the parking lot at the Muny Opera. We were chased by the cops several times. It was the first time I was smooched by a girl and thoroughly enjoyed it. One night she caught me off guard and brought a ring and said she wanted to wear it so she could show everybody that she was engaged. I should have stopped it right there but because of my unpleasant environment at home I consented. One weekend, Dr. Anderson, who was a big, jolly, humane, and well-educated man, invited me to spend the weekend at their cabin at the arboretum at Gray Summit. It was a beautiful fall weekend and it was a real treat to eat our meals outside in the fresh air. It was the first time I slept in a sleeping bag, which was a unique experience. I had driven Phoebe out in my own car so Phoebe's parents went home early Sunday afternoon and we stayed a few hours and did some more smooching. At the time I couldn't see the trees for the forest and, being madly in love, I leased an apartment from Ed Cassilly on Elm, one block from Kaegel's. My folks discovered that Phoebe was more handicapped than appeared and was not able to care for herself. Further, to put a kibosh on the engagement, Mrs. Anderson went to the hospital with angina and stayed there till I told Phoebe that it would be wise to call it off for a while. As you might expect, my mother wanted to completely cut all ties and I never spoke to Phoebe again. It was probably for the best but it was a bitter disappointment. Recently I learned that Pheobe passed away at the age of forty-four.

In later years, Chuck and I took several vacations to the upper peninsula of Michigan. We stayed at Halstead's

Bayside Resort, which was fifteen miles south of Escanaba. Their resort was right on the shore of Lake Michigan. They had a putting green about fifty feet from the lake and I spent many happy hours improving my putting game.

Their resort was run by Mr. and Mrs. Halstead and their daughter, Marilyn. Mr. Halstead butchered his own hogs and was the chief cook. In his spare time between meals he would mow their vast lawn area. Their food prices were unbelievable. The most expensive item on the menu was a huge steak with all the trimmings for $4.50. Mrs. Halstead took care of the reservations, the book work and supervised the housekeeping crew. At busy mealtimes, she would also help the young college girls wait on tables. Both Mr. & Mrs. Halstead worked from six o'clock in the morning until 9:30 at night and how they stood it for six months every year I'll never understand. Quite often when it was over one hundred degrees in St. Louis it would be seventy-five degrees in Michigan. I always enjoyed the refreshing change in temperature. One summer I became acquainted with Mr. and Mrs. Eugene Foehl. I only knew them for a week but somehow I made quite an impression. For many years they have sent me post cards from their many vacation spots, and remember me on my birthday and Christmas. When Mr. Halstead died, Mrs. Halstead put the resort up for sale. Three different persons attempted to purchase the resort but each time they failed to complete the deal because they were not willing to work as hard as the Halsteads did. Mrs. Halstead took a liking to me and even to this day has followed my life through letters and Christmas cards. I'll never forget her devotion to her help and her guests.

After I left Kaegel's, Barbara Sheppard, a former employee of Kaegel Drug, was attending nursing school in Cincinnati. For some reason she began writing to me on a daily basis and sent the mail to my office. I enjoyed the attention and always answered her letters. In about four months, she came home on vacation and asked her parents to invite me over for supper. I really had no prior contact with Barb and of course was a perfect gentleman at her house. We had a nice meal and everything went pretty well. They were Catholics and I was a Mason so this could have been the first conflict. The next night Bob and Pat Copeland, who were anxious for me to get married, invited us over for dinner and a bridge game. I never made a pass at Barb, which was a mistake I think. On the way home from Bob and Pat's, Barb dropped the bombshell. She told me she could not marry me but gave no special reason. Since she was about eight years younger than I, I foolishly offered no resistance and Barbara dropped out of my life for quite some time. In the intervening years, Barb married, had three daughters and is now divorced. A few years ago, Barb discovered, from her daughter who had attended Culver-Stockton College, that the college had established the Warren E. Gerlach Chair of Accounting. She asked her mother if that was the same guy she had dated. When Barb found out about the honor, she wrote to me and has been writing to me since that time. She is now supervisor of all nursing homes in the state of North Carolina. Recently, when she wrote to me she told me that the shortage of aides in the nursing home where I live is no exception. All the nursing homes throughout the country are having the same problem. Recently Barb wrote to me and commented on the foolishness of youth. She admitted that she had married the wrong man. In my fantasy, I surmise that she might have meant I was the right guy.

On my thirty-fifth birthday, several of the Webster Lions decided it was time that I experienced intercourse. I am positive that they had gotten my father's permission because I know for a fact my dad had fooled around before he was married. I will never forget at one Thanksgiving get-together, his brother asked him if he remembered that girl he used to visit . . . Dad was kind of abashed and quickly changed the subject. The Lions first took me to the basement of one of their stores where they showed me a porno film, so I would know what I was supposed to do. From there, we went to the Red Carpet Restaurant in Gas Light Square. After dinner, they took me to the old Roosevelt Hotel. A room had been reserved and they sent me up to the room while they stayed downstairs. When I entered the room there was a girl, which you would call a prostitute, waiting for me. She introduced herself as Melody and began to undress me. When she completed the job she started to undress herself and it was the first time I ever saw a completely nude woman, and believe it or not I reached a climax before I even got in bed. She was a small-town farm girl and she had a beautiful body. For some reason she felt sorry for me and took a liking to me. She invited me to her house and for the next three years I went to her house every Sunday night. I only told my folks that I was going over to Bill's but my Dad knew darn well where I was going. Melody lived in a small four-room house in Cool Valley. I was the only one she ever invited to her home. Every Sunday she had clean sheets on the bed and everything was in perfect order ready for action. Fortunately I learned how to keep things under control and was able to do some smooching before the final act. She charged twenty dollars, which was a real bargain considering the prices today. My friend, Chuck, always said it sounded appropriate for me to go to Cool Valley on a hot Sunday evening. The only reason I quit seeing her after three years was because she moved out of town. I want my readers to know that I am not ashamed of my actions. Every handicapped person needs a sexual release and I urge every parent to arrange some sexual experience for their handicapped child. It is a natural function and will fulfill the life of any handicapped person.

During this time, I asked Dad, "How do you become a Mason?" This is all Dad needed to get the wheels turning. You are never invited to join the Masons. You have to approach one of the members and tell them you want to become one. For weeks to come, I would meet Bill Chapman at his office at 8:00 A.M. and he would tell me what I had to memorize. Nothing has ever been written and each degree is passed on by word of mouth. Bill was the lad in high school who always sold me my lunch tokens on Monday morning. Fortunately, I had a good memory and zipped through the degrees in record time. After every degree Bill would sit in front of the lodge and quiz me. In a few months I became a third degree mason and Pop nearly busted his buttons.

While working at Kaegel's, Mother and Dad went with another couple down to Treasure Island, outside Fort Meyers, for seven weeks. During this time my good friend, Nick, moved into the house and we had a ball. One evening Nick's girlfriend, Ginna, and another girl, Pat Swank, prepared supper for us. Also, when it was time for me to get out the monthly statements, Ginna came over to the drug store and performed the duties my father normally did. When Mom and Dad returned from Florida, Mom was very disappointed that I had not missed her and I had enjoyed myself during her absence. My dad said to me, "I'll never take that woman on a vacation again."

Also while I was at Kaegel's, Mom would make my father go over and sit in Forest Park on a hot day in the summer so she could have the house to herself. One afternoon, Mom called me at Kaegel's and told me she was going to commit suicide. It was a hot afternoon and when I got home I found Mom in the attic, where the temperature was at least 140 degrees, with a rope around her neck but standing on her feet. I called the police and they rushed over and extracted Mom from the rope. They told me that she had the rope so tied that she would not have hung herself. This was one of many tricks Mom used to pull from time to time for many years.

One summer while Nick and Jack were living together they decided they needed a vacation and they didn't have any money. They got the idea of calling me "moneybags" and leaving me to foot the bill. Consequently, we drove to Branson, Missouri, and stayed at Sammy Lane's Lodge and ate in the local cafeteria. One night we all went to the bar where they sang humorous and risqué songs. I drank a Coke and went back to the cabins, about ten o'clock, while Jack and Nick drank beer with two girls until midnight. Jack said that the girls could outdrink them and to this day, he remembers the girls' names. The bar closed at midnight but the boys did not get back to the cabin until 2:30 A.M. One can put two and two together and have some idea what they were doing in the meantime. The next morning both boys woke up with a terrific headache and they sent me out for aspirin and tomato juice. On the way home I lectured them on the evils of drinking but I really don't think it did much good.

Several years before the big store was to close, Uncle Al saw that the job was getting too big for me to handle. Instead of firing me he found a painting contractor who needed someone to keep track of his time and materials and get out his bills. Consequently, he introduced me to Pete Harris, who operated a painting business with ten employees. This was the start of my being self-employed and mainstreaming myself into the business world. Although I was no longer employed by Uncle Al, he paid me to do his semi-monthly payroll for several years.

Pete Harris gave me an office space across from his desk in the middle of the store. At the front of the building was a small retail paint store, and in the rear was a spray room, where an employee sprayed whatever was required and answered the phone and did odd jobs. The young man, three years my senior, was a Spaniard, John Lopez. John and Vera had a beautiful young daughter who unfortunately fell off a bed and suffered severe brain damage. Jayne is now forty-three years old, still in diapers, unable to speak, and requires feeding. Her mother, Vera, is one of the happiest persons you would want to see. Having a handicapped daughter, John immediately took a liking to me and we had a lot of fun in the paint store and he and Vera remain true friends to this day. I have never admired any persons more than I do John and Vera. They faced their problems head on and never thought of putting Jayne into an institution. In later years, John formed his own painting business and became a very successful painting contractor. Throughout the years I have had many fun evenings with John and Vera enjoying their meals and joviality. We have taken several vacations together that were delightful experiences.

While I had my office in the paint store I brought my lunch in a brown bag. In the summer John and I would eat lunch on the concrete stoop in front of the store. Mr. Harris developed cancer and he relied on my services more and more. Toward the end of his life, I moved my office next door to the Seabaugh Upholstery Store. When I moved over into Miff Seabaugh's Upholstery Store I was required to get my own office phone for the first time. One of the Lion members had a rather influential position at the phone company and without asking me how I wanted my phone listed, he put my name with the CPAs. One evening, the phone company called me and told me if I didn't have my listing and phone changed, they would take civil action. I was completely ignorant of the mistake that was made and I assured them that I would take immediate action. My strange voice must have scared the pants off of them. Within a few minutes, two police cars came screaming up to my office. The policemen burst through the door and said, we are calling the ambulance. We got a report you are having a heart attack. I replied, "I feel fine." They saw I had cerebral palsy, laughed, and went on their merry way. Miff rented me one of his former display rooms as an office. In a few months, insurance and investment brokers, Jim McKee and his wife, Dorothy, rented the other display room and I stayed there for about a year.

Before I went to work for Pete Harris and before Nick and Ginna were married, Nick and I took several vacations together. One trip that sticks out in my mind was when we drove through the wheat fields of Kansas, stayed in Goodland and drove on to Denver the next day. We were entertained by some of the officials of the White Motor Company which had a branch in Denver. From there we drove to Estes Park and took the Trail Ridge

Drive over the mountain. From there, we wandered down to Tucumcari, New Mexico to visit Nick's aunt. She had a summer cottage about twenty-five miles from town and suggested that we use it for a couple of days. Nick had a brand new Chevrolet, of which he was quite proud. He was determined to keep any squeak out so consequently when we drove out to the cottage on a gravel road for the first few miles we went at a pace of five miles an hour. I thought to myself, "Yea gods, if we keep up this pace, it will take us five hours to get there." After traveling at the snail's pace for about a half hour, all of a sudden, Nick said, "The hell with it," and stepped on the gas. On the way home I didn't hear any squeaks in the car. The night before we left his aunt, we shared a bed. At 3:00 A. M. in the morning I accidentally rolled out, or was pushed out of bed. Nick rolled over and said, "What the heck are you doing on the floor?" Instead of helping me up, he said, "Get your ass back in bed."

My first secretary was Mary VanHook. I first met Mary when I worked in the high school office during the summers. She was Dr. Verby's secretary and the most old-fashioned girl I have ever met. She belonged to some strange religion that did not allow her to show anything but her face and her warm smile. When all the other secretaries wore modern dress, she kept wearing her long skirts to the ground and no makeup whatsoever. My next contact with Mary was at Kaegel Drug where she worked several evenings a week. Her brother always wore a hat regardless of the weather.

When I went to work for Pete Harris I still did Kaegel's payroll every two weeks. I figured everybody's salary, social security, withholding tax and so forth. After completion I took the payroll sheets and checkbook over to Mary's house where Mary filled out the check stubs and wrote out the checks. In two hours I would go back to her house and pick up the checkbook. I was always met by her bumpkin-looking father or mother who never invited me in. After Mary worked for me in the evening for about a year, I experimented and asked her for a Sunday afternoon date. I told her we wouldn't be back until eight o'clock in the evening and she would have to miss church. She went against her parents' will and I drove her to Pierre Marquette. We had a nice evening and on the way home we stopped for a milkshake. Unfortunately, when Mary handed me my milkshake it accidentally spilled in exactly the wrong place. Eventually Mary moved in with Ruth Ridgeway, the high school secretary, who didn't modernize her much. One summer, Mary attended one of her denomination's meetings in Chicago and rather quickly married a young man she met. She must have learned about the birds and bees because she raised three sons. For years, she and her husband sent me a Christmas card but always enclosed a folder telling me about why they believed in Christmas. It has become quite boring. Jim McKee then rented a building across from Kaegel Drug and I followed him and rented an office from him.

After several years on Big Bend, Jim bought a building at 118 East Lockwood. The Chamber of Commerce rented the front office; Jim used the big middle office and one of the rooms in the rear. I had the other rear room with the air conditioner in the window. There was a parking space in the rear, but in order to reach it you had to drive down a ninety-foot pathway between two buildings with one inch to spare on either side of your car. To prove my driving skills I want to tell you I never put a scratch on my car.

At one period Jim employed a blonde to do simple clerical work. She always parked her car alongside of mine in the rear of the building. One morning her car was missing and I yelled when I opened the door, "Thank God, that dumb blonde isn't here today." Instantly, Mary Batz, the secretary of the chamber of commerce, pointed to her and Jim's wife pointed to her and I was never so embarrassed in all of my life. Either the dumb blonde didn't hear me or refused to pay attention. In a few weeks Jim fired her and then things got back to normal.

My next move was to an office over Wichman's Flower Shop on the corner of Gray and Baker. My business continued to grow and for many years I worked seven days and five nights a week from January to April doing income tax the hard way. In those days we did not have computers. All figuring had to be done with your brain. In addition, I acquired five or six accounts for which I did their quarterly reports. Many of my income tax clients were former teachers, several former principals, and even one superintendent of schools. My work was quite exacting and I had to be on my toes at all times.

In my many years of preparing income taxes, I have found that the poorest people are the most eager to pay their tax and to have it prepared exactly according to the law. On the other hand, I used to prepare a minister's income tax who wanted to cut every corner he could and even corners that I wouldn't stand for. I have also known several well-to-do people who have risked the possibility of serving prison time and ruining their family's reputation just to save a few measly dollars. After preparing taxes for twenty-five years I was glad to sell my business. The person who bought my clients doubled or tripled the fee I was charging. Only then did I realize how cheap I was working, but all my clients were very content and never complained about my charges—except for the minister.

5
Activities in Various Service Organizations

Because of his father's membership, Al Kaegel, Jr. automatically became a member of the Webster Groves Lions Club. Much to my surprise, while I was still employed at Kaegel Drug, Al Kaegel, Jr. filled out an application for me to become a member. For some reason I was accepted and in March 1955 at the age of thirty-two I became a full-fledged member of the Webster Groves Lions Club. At the meeting, when I was inducted into the Lions Club, I once again spoke my mind. I told the members that I was honored to become a Lion and that I would work hard for the cause of Lionism.

My first outburst was when the other service clubs in Webster Groves wanted us to put our signs along with their signs at the entrances of the city. Many of our members thought we ought to have our own signs and ignore their request. I vehemently opposed that theory and said that we should always cooperate with everyone we could. Since I was a new member, I guess I had guts to express myself so loudly—but that was the way I felt and I never pull punches. May I proudly say I got my way.

My next incident was when I was spending a week in a tenement house in New York with my friend. They say there is safety in distance; I wrote the board of directors and said that one of the most important things we could spend our money on is the education of young people. I suggested establishing a yearly scholarship and the board accepted my suggestion. Of course, I put my foot into it. I was made scholarship chairman and served in that capacity for fifteen years. At first, we gave five $300 scholarships to any qualified student in the Webster Groves School District who applied. I drew up a scholarship application form that asked for detailed information concerning their scholastic ranking, the size of their family, their family income, their outside activities and other pertinent information. I served as chairman of the scholarship committee along with four other members who made the final decision. A few years ago that scholarship was renamed as the Webster Groves Lions Warren E. Gerlach scholarship. Currently we are giving four $1,000 scholarships.

After two years I was nominated to serve on the board of directors. There were six other older members competing for this position. For some reason I was elected and served on the board in many capacities for many years.

In 1962 my name was submitted to run for the office of third vice president along with three other older members. For some reason I won out and gained a more important seat on the board of directors. Each officer automatically moved up until they became president. It so happened that the second vice president dropped out and I was automatically installed into the first vice presidency. The new president conducted one meeting and announced that he would not be there for the following meeting. I know darn good and well that he didn't think I could handle the job and he wanted to give the members a year to select somebody else for my office. However, I showed those squirts I could conduct a meeting as well as anyone else and nothing else was ever said.

In early June, I accompanied a group of Lions to Lake of the Ozarks. We were the guest of Lion Bill McGee. While at Bill's cabin, four or five of us went for a speedboat ride on the lake. When we returned, many of the members including myself decided to go in for a dip in the cove of the lake. They put me in a huge inner tube and later I learned I was floating around in forty feet of water. When I got back on shore, one of the clowns put a fish hook down the rear of my swim suit and then struggled to get it back out. Boy, if you don't call that mainstreaming, I don't know what is.

After supper I was asked to help with the dishes. I volunteered to wash, but since I had never washed dishes in my life, I put the dishes under the running water and I thought that would be sufficient. Instantly, I was told in no uncertain terms that I was to use soap to wash dishes. This was a true learning experience.

The next year I was installed as president of the Webster Groves Lions Club and enjoyed every minute of it. For years when a new president took office the members bombarded him with wet napkins. However, one of the members had passed away during the week and when I rang the gong, I said, "In memory of our departed member, we will all say the Lord's Prayer." Immediately, I shouted, "Our Father," and that took care of that. From that meeting on I was treated with respect and never had to call for quiet.

During the weekend at the lake, one of the assistant superintendents of the Webster Groves School District approached me and asked how I would feel if he put up an African-American for membership. I told him I had no objection. Consequently, he submitted the nomination, the Board of Directors approved of it and sent it to the general membership for their approval. I was in an awkward position as president and felt that I should stay neutral, although I felt strongly on the subject. I regretted that all my education had remained very white and even our household help was always white. In our club a prospective member has to receive two-thirds of the vote of the members to become a member of the club. At the meeting, when the vote was taken, about twenty of the members who hadn't been there for years showed up to cast their vote. Someone surely must have organized a phone committee. Even with these biased older members the candidate just missed becoming a member by a few votes. To this day I have a pain in my heart for the outcome of the vote. May I point out that this candidate is now president of the Harris-Stowe Teachers College. Our club missed the opportunity of having a great leader.

The outcome of this occurrence has bothered me so much that only recently I wrote a letter to the Lions Board of Directors suggesting that any member who has not attended a meeting in a year be prohibited from casting a vote on a prospective member. In the same letter I urged that the board seek out qualified African-American members so that our club could become integrated.

My next important meeting was when the new teachers of the Webster Groves School District were invited for lunch. This is an annual custom of the Webster Lions and I applaud it loudly. I invited my old friend, Reverend MacAllister to speak before the new teachers. Since he arrived late, I had a few minutes to kill so I proceeded to tell the new teachers about what happened to me that morning. I told them that I had met a young man on Lockwood that morning who had a handicap. I asked him where he went to school and he said Webster High. I asked how he was getting along. He replied, "I am just doing swell because every teacher takes a little special interest in my development." I want you new teachers to know that this is a trait of all Webster teachers and I hope you will continue to do the same. By the way, that little guy I met was myself.

My next interesting meeting was when I invited the executive director of the Greater St. Louis Cerebral Palsy Association to speak before the club. He told the members, when it came to cerebral palsy, I was a Cadillac, and there were many, many children worse than I was. Even to this day our club sends a small check to the Cerebral Palsy Association in my honor.

The next meaningful meeting was when we invited the football team to be our guests immediately preceding the annual Turkey Day game. To keep all the members happy, we always included the cheerleaders and had an important local sports figure as the speaker.

At the meeting before Christmas, the members always exchanged gifts and we had the same Santa Claus for many years. In several years someone got the idea of dressing me up in the Santa Claus suit. When I stumbled in and started to stutter, I said, "Oh Santa had a few too many but he still wishes everybody a merry, merry Christmas." Many members regret that they didn't have a camera available. It was a moment they will never forget. Then, at the next Christmas party two of the members dressed in Santa suits and carried a sack over their backs. Of course, all the members expected one of their wives to pop out of the sack but guess who it was? It was me!

The next eventful meeting was when the club met at the new Shriners Hospital on Lindbergh Road. We toured the facilities and only then could one realize how lucky one is. The Shriners do an outstanding job and they never charge one cent for the care of the children.

In the spring of the year, one of the Lions members was an insurance salesman for Travelers Insurance Company. He was always able to obtain the film from the Masters Golf Tournament and it was an outstanding meeting. In May, the Webster Lions entertained our scholarship winners and their parents. Since the scholarship program was my baby, I took extra pleasure in presiding over the meeting. Throughout the year my voice became stronger and stronger and from that time on I had no difficulty at all in speaking before a public audience. I was sad to see my year come to an end because I enjoyed every minute of my presidency.

Every summer the Webster Groves Lions Club has their main fundraiser, a carnival and barbecue, which is held for four days at the Memorial Field in Webster Groves. Most of the members worked their butts off in hot, sticky weather. In the early days we were allowed to have gambling wheels and bingo, both of which are now outlawed. For twenty-five years I worked at the carnival all four days from the start to finish. For the first few years I sold tickets for the Ferris wheel. After each day I would go home wringing wet. Then I graduated to the air-conditioned cash trailer and prepared the cash for the opening of the carnival and stayed at night until every last cent was counted. It was the hardest work I ever did.

At this point I want to tell a funny happening. One day at the carnival, we ran out of change. I offered to drive the car if one of the members' kids would go in to the movie house to pick up the change. One of the members asked his young son to ride with me. In those days, anybody who saw me walk would not believe I could drive a car. After we returned with the change, the young boy got out of the car and said to his father, "Gosh Dad, I thought you were going to get me killed."

In addition to the carnival, when Bud Wichman was president, he suggested I write a newsletter every month. I named it the "Cub Squeal" and for fifteen years, besides writing the pertinent news, I heckled and teased every member I could. All the members say the "Cub Squeal" has never been so interesting since I gave up the editorship.

Another project that was dumped in my lap was the editorship of the annual yearbook. Besides writing the book, I spent one entire Sunday with Harry Menke proofreading. I also took one route delivering the book to every house. I would drive the car and several members' children would do the running. I would meet them at certain corners so they could refill their arms.

One of the most active members in the club at that time was Donald Bryson Gerber, the owner of one of the local funeral homes. As is customary with most funeral directors, Don is most serious while conducting a funeral service. Although he is a Protestant and a Mason, Don always tickles me when he repeats the rosary at a Catholic funeral. Don has been a lifelong friend and has been very helpful throughout my lifetime.

I imagine I am one of the very few cerebral palsy persons ever to be president of a Lions Club. In order to accomplish this feat I had to be as normal as any other president except for my physical impairment. This is an excellent example of mainstreaming.

Three years ago all my efforts in Lionism were rewarded when I received the Melvin Jones Fellow award. In over fifty years I was just the third member in our club to receive the award. Again I might say I gave Lionism everything I had.

While I was an active member of the Webster Groves Lions Club, I wrote the following essay:

The Dream That Could Become Reality

Last December, at a meeting of the local Lions Club, several of the fellows at the table mentioned that this was the week of the bombing of Pearl Harbor. One fellow told about being the lone survivor of five marines trapped in an attic, which was practically blasted away by enemy mortar. Another man relived the brutal stabbing of his commanding officer by a Japanese officer, senseless with drunken power. Still another vividly related the torture incurred in a Death March of fifteen miles in the broiling sun without food or water.

Mention of these atrocities caused me to recollect some of my civilian experiences at the time of Pearl Harbor. Being a high school senior at the time I sorrowfully remember a large majority of the boys in my class entering the armed services either before graduation or immediately afterward. Some have not returned. Then, as a freshman in college, I still can vividly see the flowing tears of relatives as they watched their boys ride off in the local army bus.

Maybe, for short periods of time, it is well for us to talk about the unpleasantness of the past. Only then can we be endowed with the gnawing desire for world peace. However, living in the past is a sure sign of decay. We Americans should forget Pearl Harbor. Look on the positive side of history and make V-J Day red letter day in American history.

Think back! Where were you on V-J Day? Did you think that this day would mark the end of all world hostilities forever?

I remembered what a few of my professors expounded after V-J Day, when hopes for lasting peace were at a high ebb. My sociology professor was dreaming of a universal government, a universal language and a universal religion. With everyone thinking alike and being able to communicate freely, how could there be another war? My economics professor was advocating stronger economic ties with all the countries of the world. With every country of the world receiving its fair share of the economic wealth, no country would waste billions of dollars on a war of annexation. My religion professor had high hopes that the forces of Christianity and democracy would spread rapidly to all parts of the world, which he felt would be a great deterrent for world conflicts.

Fourteen years later, having experienced the Korean War, the discovery of the nuclear warhead, and countless border incidents, I regretfully admit that my college professors were far ahead of the timetable for world peace. However, they were not wrong, because I feel as confident now as I did when I was a dreamy-eyed college senior that it is still God's ultimate plan to have "peace on earth, good will toward man." Dreaming about a rose-tinted future is not enough. We, as American citizens, must take the lead. No matter how great the personal sacrifice might be, we must acquire a better knowledge of the problems of the world. This is the only possible way that we can be successful in our leadership of the world. Furthermore, to assure this sound and continued leadership, it is the responsibility of every citizen to take the younger generation under his wing. We must instill in our teenagers a fervent desire for the democratic way of life, we must educate them in properly staffed colleges and universities, and above all we must conduct ourselves as Christian Americans every hour of every day, in order that the younger generation can follow in wholesome footsteps, and thereby, emerge as an even stronger generation devoted to *world peace and Christian decency* toward all mankind.

During my years in business I wanted to support my community and I became more active in the Webster Groves Chamber of Commerce. In a year or two I was mainstreamed vigorously into the activities of the Chamber. After serving on the board of directors for one year I was nominated for second vice president. In the meantime, Aunt Pearl became seriously ill and was hospitalized from January to June, when she passed away leaving a considerable sum of money in my care. Since Aunt Pearl was invited to attend the Chamber installation I smelled a rat and thought that I would be Citizen of the Year. Because of her illness I found out later that the officers were afraid I would not attend and consequently gave the honor to my good friend, John Gable. Ever since that time I swore they would never catch me off guard.

In 1970 I was installed as president of the Chamber of Commerce. In my acceptance speech I stated that since the community had been so generous in accepting me, I would do my very best to repay them. I also praised Uncle Al for giving me my first opportunity to show the public what I could do. It took a lot of guts for Uncle Al to allow me to wait on customers and to trust me with the management of the store in his absence. Uncle Al regretted that he was not present to hear me praise him.

At this time my office was over Wichman's Flower Shop and the Chamber office was right next to mine in the same building. Mary Batz was the executive director and we worked closely together. I got out a monthly newsletter and kept the members as interested as possible. At my first board meeting I challenged the treasurer, Mr. Clark, to get two hundred members to join. Since I bet him five dollars that he couldn't do it, he busted his gut and collected the five dollars from me.

Another interesting moment was when I went with Webb Rogers, an older member, to solicit new members. Webb owned a lot of property in Webster and the paint store on the corner gave him a contractor's discount. When we went into the hardware store, the first thing he said was, "I don't see why you don't give me a contractor's discount like the paint store does." What a horrible way to approach someone to become a member of the Chamber. Needless to say, the owner of the hardware store did not join the Chamber that year. On the way back to the office, Webb said, "That wasn't very smart of me, was it?" I replied, "Hell no, it was stupid."

While being president of the Chamber I made a point of attending many of the city council meetings. On one cold January night when the temperature was ten below I braved the cold to encourage the council not to initiate a sales tax before Kirkwood did. I won my point and I guess it was worth freezing my nose.

One of the difficulties of the Webster Groves Chamber of Commerce not being very forceful is the fact that there are five distinct business districts in the city. Therefore, it is extremely hard to get all five areas to participate in any sales promotions or any other joint activity.

As president, I was automatically put on the committee to select the Citizen of the Year. While being on the committee, the rule was changed that you were not required to live in Webster to receive the award. Since I lived in Shrewsbury at the time I wondered why they changed the requirement. After serving on the committee for three years when Ray Scholin was president, my secretary, Marge Wehmeyer, asked me to write a nomination for myself. Naturally, I wrote it as flowery as possible and covered many of my activities. That year when Ray

Scholin passed the nominations for me to read and to write a summary of my selection, he forgot to remove the envelope that had my secretary's home address. At the 1972 installation of Chamber officers, and the announcement of the Citizen of the Year award, Bill Chapman, who sold me my lunch tokens in high school and who lectured me in my Masonic work, was asked to present the Citizen of the Year award. Bill read the nomination and I must say it was well written. Bill ended the reading by saying that Slick Gerlach was Citizen of the Year. Of course, I was well prepared and had my acceptance speech ready to go. In my acceptance speech, I asked four questions. "Would I be here tonight if I had not had a wonderful mother and father who taught me to stand on my own two feet? Would I be here tonight if I had not had the opportunity to receive a wonderful education? Would I be here tonight if I had not been born in America where everyone has an equal opportunity? And fourthly, would I be here tonight without the help of God?" (I used this speech four or five times subsequently when speaking before my various organizations.) Of course, I got a standing ovation. After I sat down Ray Scholin made quite a speech of how they tricked me and caught me off guard. When he sat down, I pulled out an envelope with a message I had written that afternoon. It said, "Ray, I sure hope you don't ever try to rob a bank. You would be caught before you entered the door. Next time, don't forget to remove the envelope along with the nomination."

Being president of the Chamber and receiving the Citizen of the Year award is another example of the success I had in mainstreaming myself into everyday life.

Because of the publicity of the Citizen of the Year award, Emmy McClelland, my state representative, submitted and was successful in acquiring a Missouri House of Representatives Resolution which recognized my accomplishments as an outstanding citizen of the state.

After receiving the Citizen of the Year award, I was approached by a member of the board of directors for the local Red Cross and I immediately accepted an appointment to the Webster Groves chapter. I served on the Webster Groves Red Cross board of directors and they later appointed me to represent the Webster Groves chapter on the St. Louis board of directors.

The St. Louis board was comprised of many important businessmen and I was probably the youngest member. At that time the Red Cross was outgrowing its present facilities and a new building was desperately needed. All the members hemmed and hawed about committing ourselves to the expense of a new building. I took the bull by the horns and made a motion that we start building immediately. Fortunately, adequate funds were raised and the present building on Lindell was built. During the years it has served many people and has been the focal point of all blood donations. Therefore I have always been proud of my bold motion.

Shortly after my tenure on the board of St. Louis Red Cross, I was contacted by the St. Louis Cerebral Palsy Association to become a member of the board of directors. Nancy Forsyth attended the Chamber installation when I received my award for Citizen of the Year, and she convinced the Executive Director that I was just the ideal person they were looking for to serve on their board. They had been looking for a consumer to participate in the board's activities and I was selected to be their point man. Once again, I was the youngest member of the board, which was comprised of many well-known businessmen. The idea of the executive director was to load the board with influential men who could do something for the organization. I feel that the board should have a couple directors who were actually involved in the operations of running a cerebral palsy facility. However, the executive director of the St. Louis Association was a fiery, strong-willed young man and he was not about to take advice from anyone. His idea of an ideal board of directors was to rubber stamp all his activities. I learned in later years that most of his employees were unhappy and didn't dare cross him. I served on the board for nine years and was financial vice president for six years. I went over to the center once a week to sign checks. I was in line to become president but he always managed to bypass me because he knew I might cause trouble. In all fairness, Dave Young, the executive director, did a good job and saw that the clients received proper attention.

After serving on the board for several years, the National United Cerebral Palsy Association formed a consumers' advocacy committee and I was selected to become a charter member of the group. We would meet twice a year at various locations throughout the country. Each year one of the meetings would be held in conjunction with the National Convention. Therefore, my participation in this committee took me to Atlanta, Washington, Chicago, Dallas, Pittsburgh and Boston.

The first meeting of the advocacy committee was held in Pittsburgh and I know I was the only cerebral palsy member who drove the distance. I'll never forget my hotel room that overlooked Three Rivers Stadium, which got its name because it was built where the Monongahela and Allegheny rivers unite to form the Ohio River. The representative from the national office was Jim Murphy, who had a mild case of cerebral palsy. The chairman of the committee had a form of cerebral palsy but could speak well and held an important position in the business world. Another member of the committee was a judge who heard utility and other civil cases in his court. His main difficulty was walking, but he was really ahead of his time. He was married and his wife always accompanied him. Another member of the board was a young man who was married to a person who also had cerebral palsy. Both were rather disabled but they had three children. Since they required considerable assistance, I really don't know if that was a good idea. The member of the committee who was responsible for the formation of the committee had a most severe case of cerebral palsy and he always traveled with a female companion who took care of his personal and medical care. She was the only one who could understand his speech. Another member was a young, middle-aged woman who was always accompanied by her mother who really protected her. Another member was a girl in a wheelchair who could speak well. One night I was wheeling her to her room and she said she was having a party and she wanted me to come back in a half hour. Like a stupid idiot, I did not go back. Later, I found out she did not have a party and no doubt I missed out.

    Usually I drove my car to these meetings, but because of ice and snow I decided to take a train. On my first trip on the train to New York I had a most unusual experience. I went into the diner and sat down in the only available seat. As soon as my food was served, the young man sitting across from me, without being asked, grabbed my plate and started cutting my meat, buttering my bread, etc. Of course, I asked him how he knew what services I needed. He told me he had worked in a cerebral palsy facility during the last summer and was knowledgeable on the needs of a cerebral palsy person. It was quite a coincidence. We had a nice visit in my roomette after dinner and the next morning he knocked on my door and offered to help me get dressed. He was quite a guy.

When I was scheduled to attend a National Convention as part of the consumers' committee, the chairman of our committee was supposed to address the convention. Because of the Three-mile Island atomic incident, the chairman of the consumers' committee canceled his trip. At the last minute the national organization called me and told me to prepare a speech for the upcoming convention, which was only two days away. Since the convention was attended by many parents of cerebral palsy persons, I gave a short summary of my life and showed them how important it was to mainstream their child wherever possible. I told of the marvelous job that my mother had done rearing me and that she often made me feel much better, because she let me struggle to accomplish a feat that she could have done in five seconds but took me five minutes. After a round of applause the president of the organization relieved me at the speaker's podium, and she commented, "You surely had a wonderful mother."

In a year or two, trains became too slow and I went back on my statement that I would never fly. In December I was required to attend a meeting in Washington, D.C., and my business associates convinced me that I had to fly. Since my travel expense was covered, I added my own funds and flew first class. It was a very cold morning and one of my business associates drove me to the airport. They were defrosting the wings of the plane and I thought, "Boy, what a way to start flying." I told the stewardess that this was the first time I had ever flown. Bless her heart, she sat next to me during the takeoff, and I would never travel any other way from then on. When we landed in Washington, D.C., it was 43 degrees, the grass was green, and I couldn't get over the change of climate. At the Washington airport they had a passenger trolley that took you directly to the taxi stand.

After serving on the consumers' committee for two years I was not asked to repeat my term. You could say I was a thorn on the committee's point of view because I preached moderation. Most of the members thought that the world owed them everything and I thought some of their demands were quite unreasonable. For example, I don't see why all buses should be required to have lifts when only five or six persons in a big city would make themselves available to that service. It would be a lot cheaper for the public service to transport them by taxicab rather than spend millions and millions on special equipment on buses that would never be used. Another point I questioned is the insistence of converting an old building to be completely accessible to the handicapped when only a few would make themselves available for the need. Of course, I strongly favor all new construction to be built completely accessible for the handicapped.

Another outshoot of serving the St. Louis board was being chosen to represent the St. Louis organization on the state board. This was the most frustrating job I ever undertook. The state director had dyslexia and I found out that he had his assistant write all his letters. The only thing he had to hold on to was that he persuaded a wealthy man to leave a large amount of money to the organization in trust. The income from his trust paid for most of the organization's expenses and he used every trick of the trade to hold on to his job. One of his tricks was to load the board with elderly women who represented small cerebral palsy associations throughout the state. They knew about as much about cerebral palsy as the man in the moon. However, they worshipped the executive director and saw that no action was taken against him. Once, the president of the Missouri board was a young man who ran an agency in Cape Girardeau. He agreed with me that the executive director should be replaced and, along with another knowledgeable board member, agreed to have breakfast with us before a meeting so we could plot our action for the director's dismissal. Unfortunately, he chickened out and never turned up for the meeting. At the meeting I asked the director to be excused so the board could discuss our future actions. The director smelled a rat and had one of his old friends call and tell our president that no action could be taken on such short notice. Consequently, when the vote was taken, three were on my side and all the old women voted for their hero. As I left the meeting the director had guts enough to walk out to my car with me and said he was sorry about how I felt about him. Needless to say when I returned to St. Louis I immediately resigned from the board. However, I got the last laugh because several years later more competent men were elected to serve on the board and they gave him the boot in short order.

Although my work with the various cerebral palsy organizations was quite frustrating at times, it was very pleasurable and rewarding. By serving on the consumers' committee, the National organization recognized my abilities. I was asked to speak before the National Convention, which gave me an opportunity to express myself quite freely. Since many parents were in attendance, I told about the wonderful job my parents had done in making me as independent as possible. I related my speech on how Mom and Dad made me struggle to learn how to brush my teeth, comb my hair, button my buttons, etc. In addition, I gave several examples on how I handled certain situations, including the Oklahoma turnpike incident.

I also pointed out to the convention the value of education and that all parents should mainstream their handicapped child to the greatest extent possible. One of the main points all handicapped people should keep in mind is to try to act as normal as possible physically and mentally. I closed my speech by asking my same four questions that I have already quoted in my Chamber of Commerce Citizen of the Year acceptance speech.

At another National Convention a contest was held to see which local cerebral palsy association would come up with the most inventive program. Since the St. Louis association had recently opened the Marlborough House, I was asked to write the story behind our project. The Marlborough House served as a respite home. The object of the home is to take cerebral palsy children or adults in for a few days or week while their parents get a short relief from the daily routine of caring for a severely handicapped person. Since I wrote the story that won the plaque, our executive director thought it was only proper that I accept the plaque in behalf of the St. Louis association. This afforded me the opportunity to become recognized by the National Association. Consequently, I was put on several ad hoc committees and flown to New York frequently. I was always provided a room at the Warwick Hotel, which became my home away from home. It was an old hotel but it served the purpose quite well.

One of the ad hoc committees I was asked to serve on was for strengthening the state organizations. Since I had a horrible experience with the State of Missouri Association I was ready to expound freely. My idea was that the national organization should remain as it was and continue to appoint the district managers. Then I argued that district managers should play an important part in finding capable individuals to serve as a state executive director instead of being the selection of the state boards of directors, who frequently had little experience in their qualifications to recognize the proper qualifications of a suitable director. If a suitable director was found, then he could give advice to the local boards in their hiring of a director. Since our national association was growing by leaps and bounds, I felt that it should be structured as any other corporation, and the operation should be handed down from one tier to another by trained personnel. My closing argument was that too many state and local boards were composed of people who have very little experience in the operation of running a handicapped agency.

One of the other ad hoc committees I served on was the planning of the next National Convention. I still believe that a picture is worth a thousand words. I strongly urged the committee to use as much film as possible, which would make the convention more interesting. It was a pleasure to serve with the men at the top of the organization and consequently I made many friendships.

In addition to the National Convention, district meetings were held. I was asked to attend several and one sticks out in my mind. At this meeting we had a motivational speaker who talked on "Warm Fuzzies," and "Cold Pricklies." The whole object is that one person could get a lot farther in life by being happy and complimentary rather than being a cold and sarcastic son-of-a-bitch. Throughout my life I have tried to adopt this "warm fuzzy" principle; but when I do give a "cold prickly" I go all out. (My secretary said, "Amen.") After returning from this meeting I gave the identical speech before our local Lions Club.

In summation of my cerebral palsy activities, I want to say it gave me an opportunity to see this country. My commitments carried me to Chicago, Pittsburgh, New York, Boston and Atlanta. At each location I was afforded first class facilities and enjoyed the camaraderie of the other representatives. At each hotel the staff must have been given instructions on the needs of the cerebral palsy person. They really went out of their way to help us in every way possible. You will never convince me that the large majority of people are not warm and fuzzy.

The state executive director, before we had our disagreement, asked me to represent the Cerebral Palsy Association on the Missouri Developmental Disabilities Protection and Advocacy Service committee. Our federal government, in its infinite wisdom, in 1980, established a DDPAS committee in each state. Each board was made up of concerned parents and one well-known consumer. The board hired a staff with the help of a Kansas University research committee. Our office staff consisted of one director and two assistants. The object of the organization was to inspect all the care-giving agencies throughout the state and to make suggestions for improvements. Each agency was given a notice when we were coming, so naturally they put their best foot forward. We met in various cities throughout the state and had all our expenses paid for by the Federal government. One of the directors on the Advocacy board was a woman who must have been going through the change of life. She wanted the office staff to send each director a report of what they did every day and a copy of their correspondence. Of course, this would have been a complete waste of time by the office staff and quite costly. Naturally, the board voted down the asinine idea. I cannot think of one thing that was accomplished and I was kind of glad when I broke my hip and had reason to resign. Of course, it only lasted a couple of years and, in my opinion, was a classic example of the government pouring money down the drain.

6
My Family Life

The last time I spoke about my family was when we lived in Webster Acres. Three years after my college graduation we sold our $12,000 house to a man being transferred from the East for $30,000. Because of our good fortune we were able to build a one-story house in Webster Ridge. The house had a living room, dining room, kitchen, a family room, three bedrooms, two baths and a two-car garage. I had my own private bath off my bedroom and had complete privacy. It was a beautiful house, but I am sad to say I had very few happy moments there. After we moved, Dad sold his stock in Acme Paper Company to an eastern mill that wanted their own outlet in the worst way. Like the money he received for his sister's estate, he invested in mutual funds, which performed admirably throughout the years.

After Aunt Tillie died, Aunt Pearl hired a scrubby Dutch German lady named Lavanda Helmke who did everything possible including yard work. She was a jewel and deserved a place in heaven for putting up with Aunt Pearl. In spite of Aunt Pearl's money, I would go in and use the toilet and find the bowl full of urine. When I called this to her attention she would say, "Oh, I forgot." My reply was, "The hell you did, you are too damn Scotch to flush the damn toilet."

After we moved to Webster Ridge, Aunt Pearl decided to build a house five doors from us. Of course, she was alone and needed somebody to be close to her. If Mother had not been showing signs of mental illness, the situation could have been quite enjoyable. At times Aunt Pearl went out to eat with us and everybody was happy. Then there were other times when Mother got the notion that Aunt Pearl was trying to take me away from her and could become quite nasty. Mom did everything possible to keep me from visiting Aunt Pearl, but I knew Aunt Pearl needed to know that someone cared and I was not about to separate all ties, therefore I would visit Aunt Pearl on the QT. But other times Mom would suggest that we invite Aunt Pearl to go along. This was only one situation of many that were quite frustrating. Aunt Pearl's main hobby was to sit at the breakfast table every morning and figure out how much her mutual funds had made or lost from the night before. As I think back, she could have been so much more carefree if she had had more education and more confidence in herself. I do not want to dwell too long on Mother's mental illness but I must relate a few happenings that played a vital part in my life and occurred throughout my many years in business.

They always say that mentally ill people pick on persons they love the most and, by golly, she sure must have loved Dad. She could be raising hell with him and somebody would come to the door and she would say, "Hi honey, how are you, it's good to see you." Then for some reason she wanted to have the house to herself on hot summer afternoons. Poor Dad had to go over and sit in Forest Park for a couple of hours. Of course I blamed Dad for some of her problems. He should have cracked the whip and not allowed her to get away with that kind of stuff. One summer Aunt Pearl was going to spend two months with a friend in San Francisco. They had rented an apartment and all the arrangements had been made for the week and I was going to drive Aunt Pearl and her friend to Union Station. An hour before I was to leave, Mom decided I shouldn't drive Aunt Pearl to the station. Of course it was too late for Aunt Pearl to call a cab. I had the choice of going against Mom's wishes or causing Aunt Pearl to miss her train. As I went out the door Mother had a kitchen chair over her head and was ready to throw it at me. Fortunately, Dad got behind her and held the chair. An hour later when I got back to the house, Mom said, "Honey, where are we going to eat dinner today?" If you don't think that is frustrating, I don't know what is.

Another incident occurred on a hot summer night. Mom said she had to get away and took the car and off she went. We had no idea where she was going but in an hour she returned and drove the car through the garage wall. In his calm way, Dad had the garage wall rebuilt and the car fixed without making much comment. Another time Mom said she had to get away and took the train down to Hot Springs, Arkansas. In two days Mom phoned and said she was on her way back. She couldn't stand being alone. Then one night Dad was up with Mom all night trying to get her to calm down. The next morning Dad was exhausted and fell asleep in his favorite chair. When he woke up, he went in to see Mom. He found an empty quart bottle of whiskey and Mom was in a deep coma. She never drank; we don't know where she even got the whiskey. Dad immediately called Dr. Vollmar and he said to rush her to the hospital as soon as possible. They pumped her stomach and after three days of trying she finally opened her eyes. Sadly, she had been in a coma too long and her mind was completely shot. From that time on, she couldn't remember from one minute to the next and she would sit by her calendar and go over it hour after hour. It was heart rending to hear her say, "Oh God, I'm losing my mind." After tolerating Mom's condition for eighteen years, poor Dad passed away at the age of eighty-five from pneumonia. Before Dad's death he was on a machine for five days and just laid there completely helpless. I have given instructions never to put me on a machine. I'm ready to go when the time comes.

Although Mom's mind was completely gone she could still remember how to play bridge. One December evening we went over to see Bob and Pat Copeland, my lawyer and his wife, and to play bridge. After a fun evening we came home and Mom started to go to bed. She had been wearing an old silk nightgown with one of her breasts hanging out. I said, "Mom, why don't you wear one of your new nightgowns." She replied, "God damn you, can't I do anything to suit you." She ran down the hall and came back with a butcher knife. I was in my bare feet and ran down the hall to my room and slammed the door. While doing this I stubbed my little toe and the darn thing throbbed all night. In five minutes, I heard Mom snoring. Of course the next morning she didn't remember a thing about the previous night.

All during those years Mom was under the best possible medical care. She went to several psychiatrists and five times she was institutionalized for three or four weeks. While in these institutions, she received shock or insulin treatments. Every time she returned home she seemed to be like her old self. However, after a month or two she gradually slipped back to her former condition. Of course, she took all types of medicine, but I feel that if she had lived during these times when medicines have been developed to control these illnesses more effectively, she would have been more calm.

The next summer I was elected President of the Lions and went down to the Lake of the Ozarks for a weekend with a group of Lions Club members. We were entertained by William McGee, who owned a beautiful cottage on the lake. I hired a woman to stay with Mom in my absence.

When I returned, I said, "Mom, where is Laverne?"

She said, "I threw the son-of-a-bitch out."

The next Monday, Laverne went to Dr. Vollmar and said, "If you don't do something with that woman she is going to kill Warren and you will have that on your mind all your life." Consequently, Dr. Vollmar sent his nurse to the house under the pretense of giving her a flu shot. It was a knockout shot and the ambulance hauled her over to St. Mary's Hospital where she spent five weeks in the psychiatric ward. I went to court and was appointed her guardian and received permission to put her in a nursing home. My friend, Don Gerber, who operates a funeral home, put her in the ambulance with the help of one of his employees, and hauled her out to the Clayton House where she spent nine years before passing away at the age of eighty-nine. Don said he had never heard anyone scream as much as she did all the way out. After Mother was in the home a few months the head nurse asked to see me. When I took out the monthly check, the head nurse said, "I don't understand how you lived with that woman."

At the Clayton House they were forced to put her in their basement with about eighteen other patients in the same condition. Mom would sit in the sitting room with the other patients. For a while I tried to visit her once a month. Quite often she would think I was her husband.

Whenever I entered the sitting room the rest of the patients would yell, "Here comes that crazy man." Of course, everyone in that wing had no control of their bodily functions and no matter how hard the nurses tried there was frequently an odor. The nurses who worked in that wing must be headed for heaven. I don't see how they stood being around those type of people day in and day out. Finally Mom became ill with pneumonia and after being unconscious for over a week the doctor, my lawyer and I decided it was time for her to die.

At the same time Aunt Blanche was in St. Agnes Nursing Home (at that time they had a sign on the front door that said NO SHORTS ALLOWED. I often wonder if they still have such strict rules). She was there for fourteen years and I visited her at least every two weeks. Aunt Blanche was extremely religious and always had her beads in her hand. She was like many converts who take up their new religion to the Nth degree. It was very fitting that she passed away on Good Friday and was buried on Easter Monday. The funeral service was held in the chapel at St. Agnes' Nursing Home. All the old nuns attended and it was the first time I had been to a Catholic funeral with all the incense and other symbolism. At the cemetery, after the priest gave his spiel and Aunt Blanche was being lowered into the ground, he came over to me and said, "Would you want to make a contribution to the home?" I thought it was the wrong time and the wrong place to ask for money and it aggravated me to no end.

After Mom went into the Clayton House and I became her guardian I put the house up for sale. Fortunately, I sold it quickly to a friend and moved to the Georgetown Apartments. Georgetown was a village of 500 apartments with two swimming pools, a recreation room, etc. It was the first time I had ever lived alone and I enjoyed every minute of it. I became friends with quite a few of the neighbors and even at that time, many young couples were living together and not married. I went out for all my meals, usually to the cafeteria in the Yorkshire Shopping Center. One of the biggest drawbacks of Georgetown was not having a garage. I did not relish going out on icy mornings and scraping the ice off my windshield and back window. However, I survived and it taught me how the other half lived.

Shortly after I moved into the Georgetown Apartments, Aunt Pearl passed away after a long illness from January to June. St. Mary's Hospital had refused to keep Aunt Pearl any longer after being in the hospital five months so I had moved her to a nursing home where she died in two weeks. While Aunt Pearl was in the hospital I had her power of attorney and took care of all of her affairs in addition to visiting her every day.

After I received my inheritance from Aunt Pearl's estate, my good friend Don Gerber, the jovial funeral director, suggested that I join Westborough Country Club as a social member. I thought my chances of being accepted were about as close as an ice cube existing in the furnace. However, I thought, *What the hell, I'll give it a try*. So after mailing in my application, the membership chairman invited me out for lunch. Of course, this was the acid test, because my acceptance to the membership depended on his approval. At lunch I made certain to order food that would be easy for me to handle. We carried on an intelligent conversation and I showed him that I was not a complete dummy. When I got up to leave, the exit was right next to the ladies' room. In my eagerness to please, I did not pay attention to the signs on the doors. As I started to open the women's door my luncheon mate said, "You've got the wrong door." At that moment I thought my chances for being accepted as a member was about nil. However, I was accepted and enjoyed ten years of membership.

When I took guests for the first time, my waiter was Sylvester "Wash" Washington, who took me under his wing and cut my meat every time I ate at the club. The food was always excellent and I entertained friends on a weekly basis. I was very careful never to draw extra attention to myself. Although I was invited to use their swimming pool, I never did because I thought it would be making a spectacle of myself. I never attended their social functions except when they had travelogues. Every member was very friendly and treated me kindly. I spent many happy evenings at the club and it was the focal point of my social life.

This was another example of mainstreaming myself to everyday life. I feel that all disabled people, especially cerebral palsy persons, have a real challenge to be as normal as possible without making a spectacle of themselves. I have traveled to many places throughout the United States, but my most memorable was the last trip to see my friend, Jim Cutter. I flew to Frisco and Jim took a week off and showed me the town.

After living in Georgetown for about nine years, the house next door to where I had my office became available. The owner of the house required the use of the basement for a storage area. He operated a floral shop next door and built the house for his mother. When he was forced to put his mother in a nursing home, he had to find someone who didn't need the basement. Consequently, he twisted my arm and rented to me for the same rent as I was paying in Georgetown. In two years he suggested that I purchase the house at the assessed valuation which was $40,000. It was a pretty good deal and I agreed to sell it back to him whenever I moved for the same price. In the meantime I added an eighteen-by-ten-foot room in the rear, which I used for an office and sitting room. Besides that, I remodeled the kitchen, the bath, installed a sprinkler system and put on a new roof. When I moved into the nursing home, after living in the house for fifteen years, I had to live up to my agreement and sell the house back to him for $40,000 although it was assessed at $115,000. As you can see it was a poor business deal on my part and I guess I learned the hard way.

After living in the house for two years I broke my hip and required round-the-clock aides. My main and most valuable aide at that time was Flora McGhee who came in daily at 4:30 P.M., cooked my supper, spent the night and served breakfast. Flora still visits me weekly at the nursing home. When I hired her I thought she was about thirty-five years old, instead of fifty-eight. Even today she has not changed one iota and her continuous youth is quite aggravating. In the meantime, I bought her two new cars to show my appreciation for her many years of service. As for my other aides I can not be so complimentary. Some really gave me problems and their ways of living were difficult for me to fathom. Many were out to get all they could while doing the least amount of work. Of course, with this attitude and lacking education it was easy to understand why they were satisfied to do menial work. For example, once in a while Flora could come up with a lulu. When she reached sixty-five she swore she didn't have to pay income tax. She wouldn't believe me until she talked with my lawyer. One other time she went to Memphis, Tennessee. When she returned she raved about how nice the people were. I said, "Aren't the people here nice too?" One day when she was working as a housekeeper for my lawyer during the day and working for me in the evening, she came in to work one evening and said "Bob insulted me. I'm not going to work for him anymore." He always teased her and was teasing when he "insulted her." I called Bob and said, "For God sake, would you apologize to Flora. I know you were just teasing." No matter how nice I was to Flora, every once in a while she would go off on a tizzy. She would feel inferior because she had black skin.

Another aide was a thirty-two-year-old man who wore a beard and only took a bath once a week because the house he lived in burned to the ground. For over a year his garage was his home without running water. When he did bathe he went to a friend's house, or went to the local YMCA. Naturally, he had a distinct body odor and a few of my friends complained. It was really sad because he was one of the most intelligent persons I had ever met. He read constantly and had a considerable amount of knowledge in many subjects. If he had been a contestant on the well-known television game show, Jeopardy, he could have been a grand prize winner. Although he dressed slovenly, he roomed with a very well-groomed professional who was a steel salesman. I could never understand how those two were attracted to each other. They reminded me of the "Odd Couple." I loaned the two of them money for the down payment on their house, but after my aide quit working for me I thought my money was gone. But my faith in human nature was restored when his lover repaid me in full. I think I got my answer whether they were homosexuals when my aide died of AIDS at the age of thirty-six.

Another aide had worked for the Cerebral Palsy Association and treated me more like a patient rather than a normal human being. He was very interested in the

Catholic religion. He would spend hours on the phone making arrangements rather than working. His sister was a nun and he wanted to become a brother but because of age and other circumstances the brotherhood denied his admission. Whenever one of his friends was ordained as a priest, he thought it was the most wonderful thing in the world and he would go a great distance to attend the ordination. He also loved to travel and would take a leave of absence whenever possible, off and on for four or five years.

Another aide was a young boy who had a Fetish of looking at nude women. While working for me he married and he and his wife had a son and daughter. He knew his wife did not approve of nude movies but he insisted on watching X-rated movies at home. Consequently, his wife divorced him and I always was sad that he thought his obsession outweighed his value of marriage and family. I always feel that for the good of the children they could have compromised and lived a happy life.

One other aide was a tall thin girl. She was brilliant. We spent hours doing crossword puzzles. At that time she had two children by two different husbands and was divorced. Unfortunately, she became addicted to drugs and one day stole one of my bank debit cards and withdrew $1,700 all within one day. Naturally, when I got my bank statement, I had to terminate her employment. I'm glad to say she is all cleaned up and works full-time as a clerk in a major supermarket.

Another aide worked every weekend preparing one small meal and providing personal care. She would sit in the room I provided her and watch religious sermons hour after hour. She asked every Sunday to leave work two hours early so she could attend church services before dark.

The first morning of my stay in the nursing home, she barged into my room and demanded I loan her $500 for her real estate tax which she promised to pay back right after the first of the year. At that time, I had a roommate and didn't want to cause a scene, so I reluctantly submitted to her wishes. In two years, she has not attempted to pay the $5.00 installments. Once again, I have to question the value of being a devoted Christian.

7
Living in the Nursing Home

One day while in the hospital I realized I needed professional care that I could not receive at home without spending a fortune. Although, after visiting Aunt Blanche in St. Agnes Home for fourteen years, and Mother, in Clayton House for nine years, I made a vow I would never end up in a nursing home because I saw people sit in these nursing homes year after year, gradually deteriorating into helplessness and senility. Fortunately, I was able to afford a first-class nursing home and a private room, where I have some of my own furniture and wall plaques of recognitions that I have received throughout the years. If one enters a nursing home with all his mental faculties and a sense of humor and works on a project, which I am doing by writing a book, life can be very enjoyable.

On one of my outings, since I have been in the nursing home, I bought my friend, Chuck, a new car and delivered it to him. For many years Chuck kept his old Mercury and drove it until it was on its last legs. To give you some idea of the condition of his car, his personal property tax was twenty-five cents. He was completely satisfied to remain in the town and never travel to St. Louis to see me. Consequently, I solved the situation by purchasing a new Ford Escort for him. One rainy April day, my good friend, Don Gerber, and I drove up and Christine Parks, one of the nurses from the home, followed us in the new car. We left the new car at the Holiday Inn in Hannibal and drove eight more miles to pick up Chuck in Palmyra. We drove back to Hannibal. In the meantime, I had to use the urinal and when we arrived at the hotel, my crazy friend, Don, carried the filled, uncovered urinal through the lobby of the hotel. We had an enjoyable lunch at the Holiday Inn. We asked Chuck when the devil was he going to get a new car. He replied, "I don't ever intend to purchase a new car."

When we got back to Don's car, I said, "Chuck, I always wanted to give you a one-way ride and the time has come. However, if these keys fit the car next to us you can drive it home." Of course, he was thrilled to death and it made me very happy to be able to do it. So often we put off doing things for other people until we die and we don't get the enjoyment of seeing other people enjoy our good deeds.

In the nursing home one meets all types of nurses, aides and supervisors. Most of the nurses and supervisors lead a normal and average American lifestyle. However, the lives of the average aide is another story. So many of them have children out of wedlock and carouse around at night, which causes them to either call in sick or drag their tails throughout the day. Unfortunately, there is such a shortage of aides, one is rarely fired because no other aide is available to replace them. Although I am very much opposed to children being raised by an unwed mother, and I strongly favor abortion in many cases, I often question my opinion on this subject, when they bring their little kids up to see me. At that time I can't help but think, *Should I have stopped the birth of these beautiful and loving children?* I have seen more beautiful interracial children and I do approve of interracial marriages if they are in love. Then on the other hand, when I see how mischievous a two-year-old can be, I sometimes go back to my original thought. In addition I favor abortion when other people are taxed in order to support the unwed mothers and their children, and then receive additional money for each additional child they have. Therefore, my readers may make their own decision on the question of abortion.

I have been well accepted by the care-givers because I take an interest in their problems and always ask about their families and their activities. My theory is that everyone likes to talk about themselves and my approach has been very rewarding. Everyone on the staff calls me "Slick" and I keep them amused by my constant teasing and joke telling. Of course, I've one thing going for me. I am on a full-care floor and I'm about the only one who has most of his mental faculties.

One of my nurses taught me how to get something you want. She lives with her boyfriend and she wanted him to buy her a dryer. Consequently when he hesitated, she quit washing his skivvies. When he got down to the last clean pair, he went out and bought her the dryer.

One evening I told her a joke which amused her greatly. However, she said, "That's terrible."

I replied, "That's no worse than you not washing your boyfriend's skivvies."

As she left the room, I asked her, "Do you still love me?"

She answered, "Slick, I'll love you forever, but you are bad! Bad! Bad!"

Another humorous incident was when a nurse began to call me "stinkweed." I said, "Where did you get that name?"

She replied, "That is what I call my dog." I asked what kind of a dog is it, and her answer was, "A mutt."

I wisecrack with everyone I come in contact with. I believe that everyone loves me because they come back for more teasing.

Whenever an aide or nurse cares for me I always praise them for the good job they are doing and they accuse me of "buttering them up." However, I believe praise goes a long way and, no matter what they might say, they always give me good service. Every morning when two aides come in at 6:30 A.M. on their final rounds, I always say, "Good morning, you beautiful girls. How are you this morning?" They always reply, "Flattery will get you somewhere."

One morning a middle-aged aide said, "Why don't you be truthful and call me an old hag." The next morning I said, "Good morning, you old hag," and she replied, "Boy I really asked for that one. I wish you didn't have such a keen memory." That same aide on New Year's Eve asked me if she could give me a kiss at midnight. I responded, "Why sure." The next morning when I woke up I found a Hershey candy kiss on my refrigerator next to my bed. The following morning I told her, "Why don't you take your candy kiss and, by the way, you can choke on it."

Two times a week I am put on a trolley and wheeled into the whirlpool room. At that time they can lower the trolley directly into the tub and fill the tub with hot water and liquid soap, which forms bubbles like a bubble bath. One time while the whirlpool was operating I asked a young aide, "How old are you?" She replied that she was twenty-two. I asked her if she had any children and she said, "I have a girl—four—and a son—one year old." I asked he what her husband did and she retorted, "I'm not ready for that yet." Another time two young aides were giving me a whirlpool. One aide said to the other, "The man that brought up the supplies this morning offered me fifty dollars." She told the other girl, "I really don't like him, and furthermore I'm worth more than that." Unfortunately, this seems to be the standard lifestyle of many of our aides. They would rather be independent and struggle to survive rather than to seek an education and live a normal lifestyle. When I hear their stories, it makes me shiver in my boots and I wonder what hope there is for our future society. But to be fair, I must tell you about an aide who attended nursing school while working at the home. One night a relief nurse came in and said, "Slick, do you remember me? I am now an RN." I told her I was so proud of her and I constantly urge all the aides, if they show any bit of intelligence, to continue their education in the nursing profession.

Recently, I heard a sociologist claim that most things run in cycles like the stock market and the rise and fall of unions, and he predicts that we are at the low point in our morals and that when these promiscuous teenagers raise their own families, they will realize their mistakes of youth and demand much more of their children to maintain higher morals and to seek a better education. To continue this theory of evolution, in 1995 the stock market made a sensational rise, so consequently the stock market will undoubtedly fall for a few years before making a strong rebound. The same thing might be said about the environmentalists. For several years they made unreasonable demands and now they find that in order to accomplish their goals, they must temper some of their impractical demands. The same thing might be said about our political parties. One party might be in for years but sooner or later they become too powerful and self-destruct. My theory is that, like your clothing, if you hold on to it long enough it will eventually come back in style. I also believe that young aides in other countries have a better work-ethic than Americans.

Speaking of clothing and dress, the dress code of the nurses and aides is gradually changing. The nurses and aides here are required to wear white uniforms, caps and shoes. Since most other homes and hospitals are allowing very nice, colored uniforms, I am advocating for color uniforms to be worn in my nursing home. On several days during the year the nurses and aides are allowed to wear colored blouses or lab coats. Some residents, who haven't spoken a word for months, suddenly break their silence by complimenting the employees by saying, "That color is pretty." One nurse told me that when she worked in the psyche ward in a hospital, they were not allowed to wear white because the doctors thought it would be intimidating to the patients. Then, too, I have read that many doctors are wearing colored lab coats because they have found that people are more relaxed and as a result their blood pressure is lower. I am sure my nursing home will eventually change their reasoning but some institutions are so hesitant to adopt the modern professional standards.

Because of the wonders of television, I have traveled all over the world and seen many of God's beautiful creations even while I was in a nursing home. In addition, I had the experience of watching the devious proceedings and the three-ring circus of our judicial system, including the O. J. Simpson trial. I also watched the gyrations of the stock market. Then, because of talk shows, I've watched with horror a small section of our dysfunctional society. Finally, I have kept up with the news and various viewpoints of many commentators and political analysts.

I have had a lot of time to think and ponder over various subjects. I have a difficult time in deciding what is true religion. I know many people who go to church every Sunday and then do not use moral or ethical actions throughout the week. Then I know other people who rarely attend church but are always helpful and caring throughout their life. To me, this is what God intended one to do. Therefore I believe it is far more important to live a Christian life from hour to hour every day than to go to church on Sunday morning for one hour. We all know some ministers who have preached kindness and goodness for years but have done questionable things in their lifetime. Having been rebuffed by the Christian Science religion and treated very poorly by Presbyterian College while I was a Presbyterian, I have every right to question the effectiveness of a church and its ministers. Then in one other religion, advice is given on the subject of marriage and family, while at the same time the advisor is not allowed to marry, raise a family and experience the hardships of a family life. These same men have the same sexual urges given to man by God and still are not allowed to fulfill their needs just because one man says that they can't do it. Consequently many are not strong enough to check these God-given desires and end up performing immoral acts. I heard an interesting comment that there is really only one God and one religion.

I heard a very recent statement that most of my readers will fail to understand. However, before making a snap judgment, please think about it for a day or two. Get ready. Here is the statement. "There is no God, but God exists." This philosophy was expounded by a person who teaches a Bible class twice a week. One more point that came to my attention was that clapping should not be allowed in church. Some churches encourage clapping when it is appropriate. I ask you, Doesn't the Bible say, "Seek the Lord and rejoice . . . ?" Isn't clapping a form of rejoicing? A group of elders spent two hours discussing this subject. They decided not to do anything about it unless it happens again in their church.

Recently, I have pondered whether education is more important than religion. If one receives a broad education I feel that he or she would be a very influential individual whether or not he or she attends church. Now I want you to ponder this hypothetical situation. A couple lives in a tenement in New York and has one son. They have the choice of giving a thousand dollars a year donation to their church or putting the thousand dollars into a savings account for their son's college education. In this instance, I feel that sending the son to college would be more beneficial to society rather than giving the money to the church.

I also feel that the millions of dollars spent on churches' interiors (i.e. stained glass windows, plush, cushioned pews) would benefit society more if it were spent on education and on the needs of the less fortunate. In addition, regardless of one's culture, I feel that the world would be more harmonious if everyone celebrated the same special holidays and events, i.e. Christmas, Thanksgiving (Jo's question—how about Passover, Rosh Hashanah or Yom Kippur?).

At the time I wrote this book it was fifty years from the end of World War II. At that time I was a junior in college and had every thought that when the United Nations was formed it would solve all the future skirmishes of various nations. Fortunately, the United States did not rebuff the UN as they had the League of Nations after World War I. The United States has played a major role in perpetuating the life of this potential peacemaking organization. We have financed more than our share of the expenses but I still believe it is a forum for nations to vent their complaints. This belief was recently upheld by the well-known American diplomat, Henry Kissinger. Unfortunately, every country has its own culture and beliefs and until various nations learn to respect the cultures of other nations, worldwide peace will be delayed. Over the years, more and more countries have been turned into democracies, which I feel is a big step in our progress toward peace. At this time, Cuba is the only country in the western hemisphere that does not have a democratic government. Therefore, when Fidel Castro attended the recent anniversary of the United Nations he was strongly rebuffed by many heads of government. Everyone must learn to modify their strong beliefs and respect the beliefs of other cultures.

I have had time to think of the many wonderful places I have been in the United States during my life. I want to start at the Southeast tip of the United States.

I spent the month of February in a condo on Marco Island, which is at the very tip of Florida. The temperature during the day was always 70 to 80 degrees, while the temperature at my home in Webster Groves was around 20 degrees. I had a view of the sandy beaches and the waters of the Gulf. I marveled at the growth of the island. Ten to twenty years ago few people vacationed there and now every spot is occupied by rows and rows of tall condo buildings. While there, I dined at various ocean-side restaurants and devoured delicious seafood. I traveled over to Miami Beach by way of the Tamiami Highway, which cuts across the Everglades. At the time I made the journey, a drought was being experienced and I did not have the privilege of seeing alligators, etc. Another time I went to Miami Beach and marveled at the miles of hotels and motels along the beach. I enjoyed the warmth of the ocean water and loved to walk in my bare feet on the sandy beaches. On my return to my home in Webster Groves, I enjoyed seeing the Bok Singing Tower, Silver Springs and Cypress Gardens. At that time Disney World and Epcot Center were merely a dream in someone's mind.

Another remembrance is my trip to the beautiful Smoky Mountains and to the resort area of Virginia Beach. While there I experienced my first professional Bingo game where Bill, one of my college classmates and a fraternity brother, and I played for hours.

I'll never forget visiting Bill for the first time in the tenement building on Kenmare Street in New York City.

Bill Black was one of my fraternity brothers at Culver-Stockton and after attending college for two years became a professional singer with the Gene Kruppa band. I followed Bill's career for many years and spent many good times with him. When he joined the band, Bill changed his name to Clay Mundy and traveled with the band on their bus for several years. Unfortunately, it was the wrong environment and Bill became addicted to alcohol which killed him in later years. After a few years, Bill moved to New York City and lived in a walk-up tenement house in the Italian district.

When I visited him for the first time I took the turnpike from Chicago to New York. One day I was caught speeding and the highway patrolman stopped me. I told him I was on my vacation. He said, "Have a good time, but please slow down." Going through the Holland Tunnel for the first time was quite challenging and a thrill. However, I made it through without incident and started to look for Kenmare Street where Bill lived. I had to go through the warehouse district and very few people had heard of Kenmare Street because it was only two blocks long. When I arrived at Bill's house, he had not returned home from work. Consequently, I walked up one flight of steps and sat in the window sill outside the hallway of Bill's apartment. I was very neatly dressed and well groomed. In a few minutes one of the tenants in the apartment came up to me and said, "We do not allow loitering in the building." I told him I was from St. Louis and came to visit my friend, Bill. He replied, "I don't care who in the hell you are, will you please sit on the stoop outside the apartment." In about a half hour Bill returned and asked me, "Why are you sitting out in the hot sun." I replied, "Because I was thrown out of your building." When some of the tenants learned of my background, they came in and apologized for the actions of the person who asked me to leave.

Bill's apartment consisted of a small, narrow living room, a tiny bedroom, and a tiny kitchen, and a bathroom where you rubbed up against one wall when using any of the other facilities. If my parents had known the condition of where I was staying, they would have thrown a fit. However, I was happy to get away from my home environment and learn how people lived in a tenement. That summer was extremely hot and Bill's apartment had two small windows. In the next block was a grocery store that was as filthy as you would ever want to see. In the next block was a grade school where the only playground was a concrete yard with basketball hoops. However, one does marvel how some students go on to be quite successful after being educated in that environment. Recently, I read a heartwarming story in *Reader's Digest*. In one of New York's slum schools their class could not be stimulated to learn. However, when two teachers agreed to exchange classes the new teacher gave each student a challenge. In a few months they entered a difficult math contest and placed first. It just goes to show how one teacher using the right approach can turn a sour apple into a golden peach.

For many years I would pick up Bill at his tenement and we would head for New England. One summer we drove out to Cape Cod, which is very picturesque, and stayed a few days in a motel in Provincetown. It is a quaint town with extremely narrow streets and many fine restaurants. One day after lunch Bill suggested that we go deep-sea fishing. I agreed and we got on a small fishing boat and headed out to sea. I was okay going out until the captain turned off the motor and I looked down into the water. That was the worst thing I could have done. For two hours I leaned over the rail and finally acquired the dry heaves. Unbelievably, as soon as we headed back, I felt fine and ate a hearty supper that evening.

For several years Bill and I stayed in Bar Harbor, Maine, in a motel right on the ocean. It was a lovely place with a lodge equipped with a cocktail lounge and a beautiful dining room overlooking the ocean. We would sit there and enjoy lobster Newberg while watching the sunset and the fog roll in. Later in the evening the sound of foghorns was unforgettable. It was always cool and refreshing during the day and sometimes quite chilly at night. Two other features of Bar Harbor were memorable—their huge pier, big enough for a car to drive on, where people would sit on the edge and fish, and the Acadian National Park, where you could just drive almost to the top and then walk to the summit. The view was breathtaking and the sound of the waves washing against the rocks was unforgettable. On the way up and back from Maine we would make frequent stops in

Boothbay and Kennebunkport. Of course, I never thought that one of our future presidents would have a summer home in that location.

One of my other favorite summer getaways was in Vermont. Bill and I would rent a cottage in the woods close to Wilmington. It was wonderful to be close to nature and still be able to drive into town in the evening and have a typical New England supper.

However, one of my most memorable trips to New York was the year I took the train the day after Christmas and headed for New York to spend the Christmas week with Bill. One of the highlights was attending the Christmas show at RCA Music Hall. The Rockettes were dressed in their customary Christmas outfits, which were red with white fur trim. During the week, Bill and I were invited to various Christmas parties that were quite exciting. The most memorable evening of the week was New Year's Eve. Bill and I went over to the Village where we ate supper in a small restaurant that had small pane windows. It started to snow and I never saw such a picturesque Christmas scene. After we stuffed ourselves we walked over to Rockefeller Center. It was a real thrill to see the skaters on the ice, the huge Christmas tree, and the snow continuing to fall. It was another Christmas scene which I will never forget. From there, we were invited to a New Year's party with forty other people. Several of the people in attendance were movie producers, actors, and airline hostesses, along with other professional people. I was paired off with an airline hostess who was familiar with handling handicapped people and we spent a terrific evening. On New Year's Day Bill and I were invited to attend a party given by a secretary of MGM. She had managed to inveigle a James Bond action movie from the studio and it was the first time I had seen a movie shown in a private home. The next day I boarded the train and headed back home full of memories that I remember to this day.

One other trip to New York was in June. At this point I think it would be well for me to describe Bill's tenement house. It was built with iron railings and iron fences across the front. When you entered the building, the wall of the long hallway was lined with mail boxes for the forty-eight families who lived in the building. The steps were marble but worn to such a degree that the marble was actually hollowed out. One hot summer day I stayed in Bill's tiny apartment and learned a lot about living in a tenement house. Most of the tenants were Italians with typical big mamas and hard-working fathers. The mothers would do the washing in their apartments and put it on a revolving line outside their window. The smell of their cooking would permeate the building. On the weekend Bill and I took the Gray Line tour which goes completely around Manhattan. It is the best way to see New York, including the Battery, the UN Building, and the huge streamliners that dock in the Hudson River. In the evening Bill and I toured the top of the Empire State Building. It was a warm June evening with a gentle breeze blowing. From the top of the skyscraper we could see the East River on the east and the Hudson River on the west. When you looked straight forward you saw a barrage of lights for miles on many of the buildings in New York. Then on Sunday morning we started out in the car to tour New York City. It was the best time of the week to tour New York City because all the cabs were non-existent and the streets were practically empty. It was a thrill to drive up Park Avenue and see the various apartment buildings where the hoity-toity lived. The expression, "The Big Apple" always brings back fond memories. My friend, Bill, who was a really talented person, filled in for many of the MC's of the Goodson and Todson quiz shows. I am sad to report that Bill had a horrible death. He wouldn't stop drinking and the last few weeks of his life he lost all control of his bodily functions. People in the building took care of him and I always marvel how complete strangers did care and made Bill as comfortable as they could while he was dying. Unfortunately, about two years prior, Bill was awarded a disability for a nervous condition and he spent the entire check every month on liquor. I have known several people who have died in a like manner and I often wonder how they lose all control of their senses.

My memory of my father is as a pal all through my life. In a way, his life could almost be compared to Horatio Alger. As you already know, Dad only had a seventh-grade education, helped support his family and attended night school and learned accounting. He was foresighted enough to form a business which proved to be quite successful. For thirty-eight years Dad served as secretary-treasurer of the Acme Paper Company, which is now known as the Nationwide Paper Company. Right after I was born Dad joined Alcoholics Anonymous and never took another drink until his dying day. For over thirty years Dad lived with his wife, Virginia, who became severely mentally ill. He always remained calm and cool and never threatened my mother in any way whatsoever. I have never known such a tolerant person in all my life. Dad always maintained his sense of humor and gave me as much freedom as my mother would allow. Dad realized all my needs and always encouraged me to take a vacation every year and to enjoy life as much as I could. Fortunately, I believe some of his calm manners and humor have rubbed off on to me. Two of my dad's favorite comments were: "It's a good idea, but it's not worth a damn!"

and "When you don't use your head, you've got to use your feet." Dad, I want you to know I think you were the best father anyone could have and I am so happy you were my father.

Another friend whom I have fond memories of is my high school associate Robert Copeland. Bob served as my family lawyer all my life and we ate lunch together at least twice a month. Bob and Pat, his wife, raised three wonderful boys, all of whom have been very successful and are now raising lovely families of their own. All his life I feel that Bob worked too hard and deprived himself of much-needed rest. Bob developed a brain tumor that his family doctor diagnosed as sinus trouble. When a specialist removed the cancerous brain tumor it was the size of a lemon. This is an example of when one should not accept the opinion of only one physician. Poor Bob became immobile and suffered for five years before his death.

While in the nursing home, fifty years after I attended Culver-Stockton College, I returned to the little town of Canton, Missouri, and to the campus of the college. On the urging of several college officers, Don, a nurse, and I started out on a beautiful day for Canton, Missouri, the location of my alma mater. The nurse was required to give me food through my food tube. On the way up we took Highway 61, which is now a divided highway, compared to the two lane road I drove fifty years ago. However, there is a twenty-mile two-lane stretch that the state is obviously having a hard time acquiring. Probably, the owner of the land is asking an outlandish price and for some reason the state has not condemned the land. Now, the highway goes around Canton and you enter the college from the west.

Since we were early for our appointment, we drove through the little, peaceful and tree-lined streets of Canton. When we got to Main Street, the first thing I noticed was that the Oberling Chevrolet Dealership was no longer in business. In its place a game room and sandwich shop is now operated by the business department of the college. The trustees of the college provided the seed money to begin the business. Across the street was the familiar Canton Cafe and bus stop. It is now known as "The Hat Rack Cafe." One half block from the cafe is still the Canton State Bank. On the corner across from the bank is the Canton Public Library and across the street from the library is the familiar dime store. From there we turned right and headed down to the river. I noticed that the old saloon had disappeared, but to the disapproval of the college, it has been replaced by two new taverns. Fifty years ago no students were allowed on their premises. I am sure the two new taverns are so restricted by the college. As we approached the river, I was disheartened that the view had been cut off by a huge flood wall. Due to the building of the flood wall, the old Mississippi can not destroy the small town with flood waters. I was sad to see the railroad station, which I used faithfully to travel to and from St. Louis during my college years riding the Mark Twain Zephyr, was now the Tri-State Fertilizer Company. Canton is no longer accessible by train. The only public transportation is by bus to St. Louis or Quincy, or by airplane to any destination.

Returning to Main Street, I noticed that the Grand Leader where Charlotte and I had many sand storms is now called "Canton Soda Fountain." Next door, Oscar Mark's Men's Store had been replaced by Video Castle. Across from the Video Castle was the Dave Steinbeck Printing Company. For years, Dave has been the editor and printer of the Canton Weekly Newspaper. In addition, he prints local newspapers for the surrounding towns. On the next corner I was saddened to see that the old Canton Hotel and dining room, which was very popular for salesmen, had been converted into a furniture store, and the upstairs rooms were now apartments. Up the street I noticed that Rice's Market, where I shopped for the boys when they were confined to campus for sipin' wine, no longer exists. A new grocery called Nieman's, had been built. Returning to the State Bank and heading west, I noticed that the one-man barber shop, operated by ol' Matt, had been replaced by two two-men barber shops. The haircut that I use to pay thirty-five cents for is now $5 to $12 per cut. Next door, the old movie theater is now being used for a warehouse. Movies are being shown at the college. We drove by the old post office where I used to mail my laundry home. In those days you could mail a letter for three cents and now is costs thirty-two cents. In those days I mailed my laundry box home for forty-five cents and I dare say it would cost me over five dollars now. On the side street was the familiar dry cleaners. In my time one could get a pair of pants cleaned and pressed for fifty cents and a suit for seventy-five cents. Now for the same services one would cost five to ten dollars.

On the way up Lewis Street, to the entrance of the college, a new house had been built where the president of the college resides. Now, instead of entering the college from the rear, the Ada Roberts driveway leads to the front of the college. However, the one hundred steps which I used to climb twice a week or more are still used by the pedestrians. We were met at the Gladys Crown Student Center by Dr. Robert Brown, President Emeritus of the college, who acted as our host, and also by my old friend, Chuck Schaeffer. We were taken into the large dining room after all the students had left for their classes. Instead of being served one particular meal within a designated time, the students have a choice of two entrees, bread and drink at their leisure and in casual wear. In the middle of the dining room was a huge circular table that is filled with various fruits during all meals. In front of the dining room were the student lounges and a small chapel for meditation. In the basement of the student center was a bookstore and a snack shop. The snack shop is called the Cat's Pause since all the CSC's teams are known as the Wildcats. Every Friday, the college publishes a small newsletter called "The Source." Each week the menu for all the meals for each day is printed in the newsletter. Dr. Edwin B. Strong, current president of Culver-Stockton, met us for dinner at his expense. While we dined, Dr. Strong said, "Slick, I hope to establish a fraternity row behind the stadium and have all the fraternities live on campus instead of being scattered around town." Never in my wildest dreams did I think two of the houses would be built within the next couple of years, and given the names of a former student and a former president of the college.

After dinner we were given a tour of the Robert W. Brown Performing Arts Center. In the building was the art department that includes painting, sculpture, etc., all of which were never included in the curriculum fifty years ago. Then we took the elevator one floor down. Chris, my nurse, who has an elevator phobia, said, "Since we are only going one floor, I'll grin and bear it." As fate would have it, the elevator stopped between the floors and it was about five minutes before the elevator started again. On the lower floor we were treated to an everlasting memory. We entered the music department and to my delight the students were preparing to rehearse. About three minutes before the class was to begin, every student began to hum in unison. Then the music professor entered the room and took his place in front, raised his baton, and the students began to sing sweetly and gracefully. I could have stayed there for hours but we had to continue the tour. One thing I did notice was everyone dressed casually and one had on a baseball cap. At the time I thought it was rather rude but, on further contemplation, I thought maybe he'd had chemotherapy and lost his hair. This was a good lesson in sociology of not judging before knowing all the facts.

Our next stop was to the new Herrick Business Center, which in my day was the old gymnasium, and the entire business department was taught in one room in the administration building. Now the building has various classrooms and an accounting lecture room with tiered seating. Adjoining the classroom is a laboratory with many computers. When I took accounting, calculators and computers were only in the minds of the makers. We used our brains to add, subtract, multiply and divide. I was especially interested in this department because a Chair of Accounting has been established in my name and the money from my trust will be used to support this department upon my demise. The new gymnasium looks like a huge dome center. It is called the Joe Charles Gymnasium because he contributed the majority of the financing and supervised the construction. At this time it is the only building on campus named after a former student.

My nurse rolled my wheelchair across the quadrangle. As we crossed, I was heartened to see that CSC was beginning to be slightly integrated. As I looked back toward the administration building, I thought of Dr. Lacey Lee Leftwith, my old sociology teacher. He would have said, "I told you so." The minorities are now coming to the forefront. We have black males and females in the armed services, holding important positions in large corporations, in Congress and one black male almost became a candidate for president. Also he would have gloated to know that we now have a white female, Sandra Day O'Connor; a Jew, Ruth Ginsburg; and a black male, Clarence Thomas, as judges on our supreme court. Lacey Lee would also be pleased to know a black female is president of the elite Smith College for Girls, and the famous black female poet, Maya Angelou composed and read her poem at President Clinton's inauguration.

It was a warm breezy fall day and the leaves on the trees were all colored and the view overlooking the Mississippi River was breathtaking. We went past the girls' dorm, which is now called Johnson Hall, and started down the small incline toward Wood Hall where I lived the two years I was in college. When I attended the college there were five small cottages along the way reserved for various professors to live in that are no longer existing. They have been replaced by the magnificent Carl Johan Memorial Library. In my day the library consisted of one large room in the administration building. From the library we went on down to Wood Hall. Three husky-built students came and cheerfully lifted my wheelchair into the lobby. I went down to the end of the hall to Room #5 where I spent many days and nights of my life. The hallway is now carpeted when all we had were wood floors, and where many of the boys use to roll Coke bottles from one end to the other. You can imagine how that used to irritate the housemother, especially when it was done around midnight. My old room is now carpeted, there is a bunk bed that replaced the two iron cots. There is a phone and a television set. Now that is a change from when I lived there because we didn't have phones nor were TVs invented. Maybe if television had existed, I probably would not have been so studious.

Down the hall, I poked my nose into the bathroom. Gee, what a change. All up-to-date toilets and individual showers rather than one tin enclosure with three spigots for showerheads where Chuck and Don used to aim cold water at me.

I marvel at the progress the college has made. Now instead of having four buildings it consists of many new buildings, including various separate boys' and girls' dorms. The tuition and board is now about twenty-five times the $500 I paid in 1944. Also, the enrollment has increased from 250 to 1,200. After leaving Wood Hall, we worked our way back to the performing arts center where we sadly said good-bye to our host.

I have been rewarded for all my perseverance and dedication to causes that I firmly supported all my life. My first surprise was when I learned that the president of Culver-Stockton College wanted to bring all of the fraternities, which were scattered throughout the town, on to the campus and form a fraternity row. He wanted my fraternity to lead the parade. However, the actives of my fraternity rebelled because they did not want to abide by the rules and regulations set down by the college pertaining to the hours when females could be in their fraternity house. I wrote a strong letter reminding the actives that when they graduated from college they would have to move into a community and abide by the rules established in that area. I thought my name would be mud but after much discussion by the actives and after three votes they decided to take the lead and move onto College Hill and be the first hall on fraternity row. Lo and behold they requested the board of trustees to name the new fraternity house the Gerlach Hall. Naturally, I was very honored and this proves that when you think you are right you should stick to your guns, and frequently you will be rewarded.

My lifelong friend, Jim Cutter, wrote and reminded me that only fools put their names and faces in public places. I replied, "Many wise men fool around and become unknown in the ground."

My sociology professor, Lacey Lee Leftwich, always said, "Your contribution to society is how you will be remembered after you are dead."

I am proud of these awards and they have made me feel that my life has been very successful.

My second shock was when the board of directors of the St. Louis Cerebral Palsy Association recognized the many hours that I had put in by serving on the local and national committees and board of directors. Consequently, they established an annual award to be known as the Warren E. Gerlach Merit Award. The award reads: "In grateful recognition of your dedication, commitment, and service, which has led to the advancement of independence and greater opportunities for individuals with disabilities and their families within their communities." I was so overjoyed when the first recipient was John D. Kemp, Executive Director of the National Cerebral Palsy Association. John was born without arms or legs and operates with two artificial arms and two artificial legs (and you think you have troubles!). It was amazing to see him hold a fork and to pick out a small piece of paper from a hat containing the names of about 250 people who attended the meeting and were being selected to receive an attendance prize.

I am now seventy-two years old and, having been born with cerebral palsy, I have lived about twenty years longer than the average cerebral palsy person. Although I am still full of piss and vinegar, I know that my time to pass on the Great Beyond could be tomorrow or a year from now, or hopefully longer. I was blessed with loving, strict and determined parents, wonderful health, good friends, and a God-given intelligence. I have no regrets about my life because all through my life, in school and in business, and in the many organizations that I have served, I have given everything I have. I want my readers to know that I will die a happy man and have no fear of the future. I believe in the goodness of God and, since he gave me the faculties to lead a useful life, I know he will take care of me in the future.